THE UNCONVENTIONAL ENTREPRENEUR

Launch a Successful Business & Live the Work-Life Dream

Alexandra Nolan

Dunleith
Publishing

ISBN: 979-8-218-04871-6 (hardcover)
ISBN: 979-8-218-04874-7 (ebook)

Published in 2022 by Dunleith Publishing
www.DunleithPublishing.com

First edition 2022

Cover Design by Margaret Carter

Printed in the United States of America

This book is dedicated to my loving husband, my sweet little boys, and my brother, who in his death, has inspired me to seize every opportunity. For you little brother, I shall live. I love you all so very much.

Jeremiah 29:11

Alexandra is the kind of entrepreneur who leaves nothing on the table. Her creative spirit and ferocious drive are evident in all that she does. She's unique in her desire to see all entrepreneurs thrive — she sees community where others see competition and happily shares her toolkit with generosity and optimism. SHE Media is fortunate to benefit from Alexandra's brains and brawn. I'm confident that many more burgeoning businesses will grow with the help of The Unconventional Entrepreneur. **Samantha Skey | CEO SHE Media**

Alexandra has given me the confidence to launch my very own business. I love her willingness to share all that she has learned. I feel so much more prepared and knowledgeable and know that I can and will be successful. **Brittany M. | Retail Entrepreneur**

We have been blown away by the growth our business has experienced after working with Alexandra. Not only the ROI, but the amount of relevant information Alexandra has taught us from her experience + knowledge in business development and marketing intelligence. My partner and I couldn't be more appreciative. Investing in Alexandra to take your brand or business to the next level should be a requirement. **L.D. | Retail Entrepreneur**

As a new stay-at-home mom exploring business ventures, learning from someone with so much knowledge and experience within the industry is an exciting opportunity. Alexandra communicates information exceptionally clearly and efficiently, adds excitement, and uses relevant examples to make connections to the real world. I feel I have a solid foundation. **Lauren P. | Entrepreneur**

CONTENTS

I

THE MAKING OF AN UNCONVENTIONAL ENTREPRENEUR

Entrepreneurialism is not a new concept, yet vastly changing business environments due to extreme economic changes and the progressive world in which we socialize have together blurred the lines between consumption needs and lifestyle attainment for consumers. In order for entrepreneurs to be successful, they're having to adopt unconventional strategies and business practices. The traditional entrepreneur has completely gone out the window and a new type of leader is taking the stage.

WHY THIS BOOK? WHY NOW?

According to Forbes, "More businesses are being launched than at any time in the past decade, and existing startups are showing rapid acceleration." Forbes attributes this to the sudden change in consumer needs and the small business capability to meet these demands. Our current market environment is allowing startups to seize new market opportunities and become more innovative with their products, services, and distribution. Furthermore, Forbes' research shows that "In Q [uarter] 3 2020, there were about 1.5 million new business applications. That's a 77% increase from Q [uarter] 2 and more than double any quarterly report from 2004 to 2017." The pandemic has put our economy in a state of creative destruction. While this sounds like a downward spiral, it is quite the opposite. This disruption has made way for new and creative business ideas to come to the forefront. The number of business startups is off the charts.

Now, let's take this one step further and two hundred steps back into the 1800s before there was corporate America and the bustling life as we know it today. Two hundred years ago, people made their own way by discovering their skill set, perfecting a trade, and turning that trade for a profit of some sort. I say some sort because some would make money, and others would trade to get the things they needed, but nonetheless, people had to build some sort of enterprise to survive.

One may beg to differ, but I am of the belief that entrepreneurialism is innate in all of us. It is a basic survival characteristic that is developed through practice and strengthened through determination and confidence. We all have a skill that can be monetized. It is discovering that skill and then knowing what to do with it that makes a life-changing difference. So, what does all this fancy language mean to you? Plain and simple, entrepreneurialism lies within all of us, we just have to know how to activate it.

If you dream of becoming your own boss, gaining more work-life freedom, and truly doing what you love, now is a better time than ever to invest in yourself, build a brand, and start your own business. That's where this book comes in. There are millions of books out there about entrepreneurialism, but with the evolution of the business landscape, so comes the evolution of the entrepreneur. There really is a difference between the traditional, by-the-book entrepreneur, and one who challenges the way business success is achieved. An unconventional entrepreneur chooses an endeavor that they are passionate about while finding ways to turn a profit doing so. Living out your passion daily on the job, allows you to genuinely enjoy every aspect of your work, reach a higher level of achievement, and attain the work-life dream. An unconventional entrepreneur knows that an impassioned and successful work environment will not only fuel creativity and freedom within work but in all aspects of their life as well.

In this book, I am going to share so many things with you. Only because many have insisted that I tell my insanely unconventional and somewhat embarrassing story, I start out by telling you a little bit about my journey. Then, we will get into Part 2, the reason why you have picked up this book. The first order of business is to discover your skill set. To me, this discovery process is one of the most exciting parts of building your work-life dream because you will reveal to yourself an inherent gift, something you are truly good at. Yes, we are all badass at something but many of us live our entire lives not knowing what that "something" is, let alone trying to capitalize on it. You may already know what your strengths and skill set are, but I urge you to read Part 2 thoroughly and participate in the exercises. You are likely to learn something that you didn't already know about yourself.

Once you have a solid idea of your strengths and weaknesses within the eight elements of an unconventional entrepreneur, in Part 2, we will discuss determination and confidence. These are two very important attributes to master before putting your skill set into action. Every entrepreneur must perfect determination and confidence to succeed in an unconventional entrepreneurial world; lucky for you, each and every one of us possesses both of these attributes, we just have to master them. I like to say, "When the going gets tough, the tough get determined." As a now-established unconventional entrepreneur, I ride the blissful waves of freedom, flexibility, and profits *(most of the time)*; however, this comes with a price. Just like most full-time jobs, every entrepreneur starts off on the low end of the totem pole. This means that you must work your way up, building your brand, executing a business strategy, and growing a loyal audience or customer base. It takes determination, a lot of determination. You have to be able to look adversity in the eye and say, "Not today, Satan!" You have to be able to remove the thought of failure, from your mindset. You have to be able to only look forward and not linger on, but learn from, past hiccups, losses, or hindrances, which will distract you from overall success. Determination will help you to achieve all these things, but determination alone cannot convert to success without confidence. In Part 2, I will also reveal how to attain and build upon your confidence, which will naturally boost determination. When you are confident in yourself, your worth, your trade, and your knowledge, you will be determined to reach success.

Once you have a solid understanding of your strengths and weaknesses among the eight elements, in Part 3 you will begin to brand yourself and your business. Yes, I say "brand yourself" because the old way of branding is obsolete. Traditionally, a business would create a product or service, brand that product or service, and go to market selling the benefits of their product. Today, people are less interested in how a product can benefit them, and more interested in how the person behind the product can provide a solution. This idea stems from social connectedness. Psychology researchers Richard M. Lee and Steven B. Robbins define social connectedness as the experience of belonging to a social network or relationship. With the advancement of the digital world, people are able to satisfy their personal need for social connection without actually being in physical proximity to one another. People are more interested than ever in knowing each other's stories. This curiosity often results in a connected feeling to the person behind the story. From a business sense, people want to know more about the person behind the brand so that they can conceptualize how the story and product fit in with their interests. This helps to form their attitude towards the overall brand. In order to avoid brand disconnection and the need to rebrand down the road, this concept must be understood. When you brand yourself on the front end, your business is able to mold and conform as your story grows and, more importantly, is able to fit into the story of those who have socially connected with you.

Remember when I said that confidence is one of the traits that must be mastered to take your entrepreneurial journey to the top? In Part 3, you will also get to put your confidence into practice. A huge part of getting your brand out there is how you personally introduce your brand to potential customers, investors, and the market in general. Just like an award-winning choir must perfect its pitch, so too must the successful entrepreneur. The most successful unconventional entrepreneurs can seamlessly brand themselves at a moment's notice to seize a potential opportunity or capture the attention of a prospective client.

When I was a young entrepreneur, I wrote a blog post about hustling as a business owner. While I was very proud of that piece, my perception of my profession was skewed. In my entrepreneurial development, I have come to realize that the word "hustler" attaches a negative connotation to our work.

hustler - an aggressively enterprising person; a go-getter
     (Oxford Lexico)

While it is true that an entrepreneur is a go-getter, an unconventional entrepreneur is not an aggressively enterprising person. Instead, an unconventional entrepreneur can quickly spot an opportunity and harmoniously engage with their target in a genuine and mutually beneficial way. In other words, the unconventional entrepreneur prioritizes mutually beneficial opportunities and suggests win-win partnerships, which naturally diffuses the aggressive characteristic of a hustler and enhances the "go-getter" trait. This is done through the "pitch," in which you quickly and creatively introduce yourself, your business, and your unique offering in as little as twenty seconds. This absolutely takes a lot of practice and confidence in order for your pitch to become second nature and eloquently flow from your tongue in a natural way, but by the end of Part 3, you will have your pitch formulated and ready for implementation.

Once you have an idea of how you are going to arrive in style to the business world, the next step is to set your goals so that you can get the job done. In Part 4, you will learn unconventional goal-setting strategies to ensure that you keep your eyes on the prize and never tip the scales. Every successful person has set goals and then implemented strategies toward achieving those goals. I am willing to bet that they have also placed unrealistic expectations on themselves at times, which has then led to unattainable goals and constrained work life. Some of the main enticements to entrepreneurialism are the joys of flexibility and freedom inside and outside of the workplace. Have you ever seen "Lady Justice?" Lady Justice is a statue of a woman holding scales, depicted in many courtrooms and attorneys' offices. There is detailed meaning and symbolism behind the statue, but overall, these scales represent the importance of balance in the judicial system. When I think of work-life balance in the business world, I immediately envision this statue with family on one side of the scale and business on the other. This vision helps me to instantaneously remember how it is so very important to strive for balance on the scales. Because unconventional entrepreneurs view their business and their passion as one and the same, it is much easier for the scales to tip in favor of business. Before we know it, years will have passed and we will have grown distant from the ones that we love, even when they are in the same house. In this chapter, you will learn how to set attainable goals for personal and business growth and tips for maintaining a healthy equilibrium so that you can keep those scales balanced for maximum productivity and work-life balance.

In Part 4, we will also talk about, monetizing your product, service, and expertise using the P.R.O.F.I.T. Cost Process, quite an enticing topic. Who doesn't like money in the bank? The number one struggle that a budding entrepreneur, and even business owners who have been in practice for years, have is realizing their worth psychologically. It wasn't until I was in business as a makeup artist for several years that I realized I had been undercharging for my services. I knew what established makeup artist professionals in my field were charging, and while early on I was working with magazines and celebrities, I still felt new to the game and didn't view myself as an equal. During the week I was in magazine shoots or doing makeup for events while on weekends, I was completely booked with weddings, driving all over town with my makeup kit in hand. What's wrong with this picture? I began to grow resentful of my job because I was underpaid and giving up my much-needed weekend family time. After two years of this, I had officially run myself into the ground. Because my weekends were saturated with clients, extra time was non-existent and my passion for the job and my relationship with my family began to suffer. I was turning out tons of happy customers but didn't feel the monetary return was equitable. No one's fault but my own.

After much thought, I decided not to give up on my dream business, but instead to devise a plan which would free up time, put more money in the bank, and revive the passion that had once fueled my creativity and work-life dream. That plan was to set boundaries and charge what I was worth, something I should have done from the beginning. I was nervous to raise my prices to match my growing level of expertise, but to my surprise, my business never missed a beat. I was able to free up some time by going from four wedding parties on the weekend down to two and increase my profits by charging what I was worth.

Traditional entrepreneurs generally focus on the fixed and variable costs associated with business activities and production operations when pricing for profit. However, while it is not yet widely practiced to assign a cost to your expertise, an unconventional entrepreneur understands that there is value to be found in their unique ability. The P.R.O.F.I.T. Cost Process was designed for entrepreneurs to evaluate their production, overt *or variable*, fixed, and professional impact costs while considering competitors' pricing structures and building healthy profit margins.

While a savvy financial strategy is a must for keeping your business profits coming in, an omnichannel strategy is essential for staying competitive in the marketplace. A company that is not embracing the omnichannel strategy to create the optimal brand experience for its customers: is simply falling behind in today's business landscape. There are so many ways to conduct business and capture conversions beyond the traditional brick-and-mortar store. Think pop-up shops, digital showrooms, websites, phone apps, QR codes, social platforms, SEO retargeting, beacon technology, email newsletters, brand events, blogs, home parties, and many more. Today, it isn't enough to merely establish a location for your business and wait for the customer to come to you. By assessing your target demographic's social habits and preferences for consumption, you will be able to devise an omnichannel strategy that meets your customers in their environment and makes your products readily available for purchase at a moment's notice.

In Part 4 you will also learn the importance of "building your village" for support, growth, and novel business offerings. In many traditional business settings strategy is comprised of business growth from a singular, internal viewpoint, often overlooking the value in mutual partnerships for leveraging customer databases, complementary services, and added expertise. An unconventional entrepreneur understands that not only can they build power and competitive edge through external mutual partnerships, but they can also create innovative solutions for their customers and the community in which they operate. Throughout the book, you will come across some callouts. Some of these are shout-outs to those who have made a huge impact on my journey as an unconventional entrepreneur and others are called "Unconventional Wisdom." The unconventional wisdom axioms are raw, transparent reflections and hard lessons that have been etched into my psyche throughout my business journey. Some may seem more obvious than others, but each and every one of them still stands with me today. Over the years some of this wisdom has transformed from simple thoughts into my personal business culture, to words to live by in the business sense. I invite you to adopt these Unconventional Wisdom axioms into your discipline. However, if these expressions just don't resonate, I encourage you to thoughtfully create your own code of Unconventional Wisdom to help guide you through this exciting journey.

FROM BARHOPPING TO BAR-RAISING

Before I get into the inspirational, motivational, life-changing stuff, I think it is important to tell you about my professional and not-so-professional background. We have all been there, our early 20s. The late-night clubbing or barhopping after work only to roll out of bed at 7 a.m. and make it to your 8 a.m. shift ten minutes late. I guess making it to work, even if I wasn't on time, shows some sort of responsibility, right? This may be an extreme example and maybe 50% or more of us in our 20s were a little more responsible with what we did in our spare time, but this example is truly the beginning of my story. In my 20s, I went to school during the day, managed a makeup counter at Macy's three days a week, and was a bartender at a downtown beer joint, often working until 3 a.m. three other days. I had one day a week to recharge just to do it all over again. While it seemed like a Jekyll and Hyde lifestyle, I loved it. Every hat I wore at that time satisfied some sort of internal need. School satisfied my need for knowledge. Running the makeup counter was great for fulfilling the entrepreneurial yearning inside. And well, being a bartender satisfied my love for good pay and social settings. While this lifestyle was one that I am not sure I could uphold today, I learned something about myself, and that is I am an "eat what you kill" kind of gal. Theoretically, you can't eat if you can't hunt. It was during this period in my life that I began to realize I could achieve my desired lifestyle if I seized every opportunity and kept hunting. While it may seem overly dramatic, this was a period of enlightenment for me when it came to realizing my potential and all that the world had to offer.

◆ ◆ ◆

Unconventional Wisdom
You can't eat if you can't hunt.

◆ ◆ ◆

I have been told by everyone who knows me, "There is no gray area with you. No in-between. You are either black or white, high or low, go big or go home." Let's just say, in my early 20s, before having children, I wasn't wasting one minute of my life on mediocrity. I was going big and then going home, sometimes a little more clumsily than I left, if you know what I mean. But while living it up, the bigger picture was always in my sights. Internally I felt called to do something different but wasn't sure what that calling truly was. Eventually, I graduated college and started a career. While working a salaried 40-hours-a-week job was new and exciting enough, I dabbled in many other things to continue to please those internal needs. I did bridal makeup on weekends, started my own cosmetic line, styled fashion shoots for a local magazine, and even tried to brand a handmade soap line which tanked quickly after launching.

◆ ◆ ◆

Unconventional Wisdom
You can't win them all.

◆ ◆ ◆

This was a time in my life for self-discovery. Initially, I thought that staying busy was the only way for me to be happy, but upon a further understanding of myself, I realized that I was lacking in work-life fulfillment. I loved my corporate job, but I just knew that it wasn't what I was made to do. It wasn't my calling.

I identify with being a bit unconventional in my lifestyle, not really rejecting, however not really following, the norm. Idea cultivation and being surrounded by men and women who can think for themselves is an environment in which I thrive. I am strong in my positions, but always welcome the visualizations of others to help shape and develop my own thoughts.

Maybe the word "unconventional" is uniquely my lifestyle, but something tells me there are others, like yourself, who feel the same way, yet I find that story is rarely told. If you research successful people *(as we should always do to benchmark our own successes)* you'll find extremely impressive, yet unobtainable examples. Stories are plastered all over the media of those with perfect upbringings, who are insanely, if not genius-level, smart, have degrees from Ivy League schools, and spend a questionable amount of time focusing on their business. Don't get me wrong, I am in no way downgrading their unique qualities or hard work. I only point out these types of stories because they can easily create insecurities in those who have not been offered the same opportunities or who are not blessed with the same extraordinary skill sets. I used to insecurely ask myself, "How can I match this?" I would say I am smart, but certainly not book smart, spending an ungodly amount of time studying to be an A or B student. I was blessed to be able to go to college, but not Ivy League. And while I truly enjoy planning for and running my business, I prioritize my role as a mother and wife.

"Unconventional" is a tough group to classify yourself in mentally. You have all these ideas and aspirations that match those around you who are wildly successful, but you question if you are smart enough or if your ideas are novel or feasible. You daydream about all that you want to achieve, the businesses you would launch, or the dream home you would retire in, but the insecurity of not being "cut from the same cloth" as those other unattainable, successful people holds you back. I completely understand the feeling. This is the very feeling that almost held me back from every opportunity that would come my way.

While working for corporate America I launched many side projects, one of which seemed to gain steam. Remember the makeup line I mentioned before? The at-home makeup parties for work colleagues, friends, and family, along with weekend bridal makeup slowly grew into a steady, part-time gig and eventually, landed me some consignment counter space in a local boutique in Memphis, Tennessee.

"To Erika, the owner of Stock and Belle, formerly Crazy Beautiful Boutique. Your kindness, support, and belief in my tiny little makeup line gave me a start physically and the confidence mentally that I needed to begin this incredible entrepreneurial journey. From one small, female-owned business to another, thank you, my friend."

Having my makeup line in a real shop was a five-year business goal; however, securing the deal took a lot of confidence building on my end. I was terrified that my community and peers would not like my new products, and even worse, feared that Erika would give me a "sympathy yes." You know, the yes you get when someone really doesn't want to say yes but they feel bad for you? The thought of chatting with Erika about the possibility of housing my cosmetic line in this popular local shop gave me a wave of anxiety, but as the old saying goes, "You will never know unless you ask." And so, I gave myself a pep talk and asked. If you can relate a bit to these internal struggles, you are not alone. Confidence is something that many budding entrepreneurs lack. Don't worry, we will go over tips for confidence in a later chapter. Oh, and by the way, Erika said yes!

I began coming into Erika's boutique a few times a month, standing by my makeup counter space, offering complimentary lip makeovers and eye shadow revamps. It was super scary to throw myself out there in the beginning, but I took this time to perfect my pitch *(another topic later in the book)* and build my brand as a professional. I knew I wanted to be seen as classy but not too perfect, a "line walker" but also respectful of the rules, unapologetically me without putting off others. I just wanted my brand to have a hint of vintage class with a little modern-day, boss-woman badass.

The makeup line slowly continued to grow over the next few years, which led me to the point that every part-time entrepreneur hopes to get to, the big decision about when to quit my job. Such a liberating, yet super-scary time. My cosmetic line was not making enough money to replace my salaried job, yet my salaried job was restricting the time I needed to excel in my small business. It was time to decide, take the leap and major risk to invest in myself, or sit on the edge of the fence, peering over at what could be. On October 15, 2012, I wouldn't just walk on the line, I would apprehensively step over it and begin a very exciting journey into full-time entrepreneurialism.

Within a seven-day span, I came up with a boutique makeup parlor business plan, signed a commercial lease within walking distance from my apartment, put in my two weeks' notice at my corporate job, and began working on getting my shop opened. I had only $10,000 in my budget for this project and needed to get my store up and running in 14 days to take advantage of the upcoming holiday season. I am so thankful that I had my family and friends who showed up to demo the old tanning salon space that I had rented so we could turn it into a quaint little shop. Shockingly, with the help of so many, I was able to hit my 14-day deadline and transform a six-room, 10-year-old tanning salon into a savvy, chic makeup boutique.

Although I had a very minimal budget *(I would never recommend starting with a budget as small as I did)* the launch of The Ivory Closet Boutique was surprisingly successful. Being choosy on the location really paid off as The Ivory Closet was the only shop in my small island community. Keeping prices obtainable was another huge strategy. The neighborhood in which the boutique was located consisted of both grad students and upper-middle-class families; therefore, there was a sizable stretch in the price points that each demographic would be attracted to. Understanding my market and strategizing accordingly really helped. These strategies weren't rocket science or anything. I just applied logic and my understanding of basic business marketing tactics to come up with a plan.

"Special thank you to my sister, Holli, who was also just getting her construction company, Hardhat Construction, up and running in 2012. She took time out of her own busy business planning to help me get my dream business ready for opening. You are such a huge part of my business journey and life in general. Glad to have you by my side. Here's to doing life together since before we really even knew what life was. Love you to heaven and back, and back again!"

Back to that budget. Remember that I said it was a pretty small budget for opening a brick-and-mortar retail store? "Small" is an understatement. For the first year, I worked in my shop, with no employees, seven days a week, nine hours a day. For the first three months, I put almost all my profits back into the store to grow inventory. This made money for marketing super scarce, yet the only way to grow was to market myself. It became evident that I needed to find a way, preferably a free way, to spread the word about The Ivory Closet. What better way than to turn to digital media? Thus, The Ivory Closet blog was born with corresponding social profiles, to share all our new items coming in weekly. After working nine hours on the floor daily, I would spend a minimum of two hours after closing posting on the blog. These two hours consisted of taking product shots and selfies with new items, uploading them to the blog, attending to the online shop and social sites, and fulfilling a few daily online orders. I wasn't a mother or wife during this time so I didn't have major priorities that would restrict my working hours; however, as you can imagine, holding every single title required to run a store was quite exhausting.

◆ ◆ ◆

Unconventional Wisdom

If you are going to make it as an entrepreneur, keep one thing in mind, nothing is beneath you. Let your moral compass be your guide. Determination, even in the midst of hopelessness, is key. And always keep your eye fixed on the end goal.

◆ ◆ ◆

About four years into running my shop, other brands began reaching out with requests for blog post reviews on their products. Becoming an influencer was not an initial aspiration of mine. Actually, I had never even thought about this professional path or really understood what it meant. My initial reaction to these brand requests was "Hell, no!" There was no way that I was going to cannibalize my own business of four years, which I had worked so hard to build, by promoting substitute products. As the requests kept coming in, my mindset began to change. I realized that this could be an opportunity, the next step in my entrepreneurial journey. By this time, my shop had become somewhat of a Memphis staple and the word about my online store had gotten out. The blog itself really didn't really need to be The Ivory Closet-specific anymore. Rebranding the blog and sectioning it off from my store could be a lucrative business move, an endeavor that I would ultimately oblige.

As you all have probably learned by now, I switch lanes pretty quickly. Within a few weeks of making the decision to become a blogger, I had researched the digital creator industry, rebranded my shop blog into a full-blown digital creator business, City Chic Living *(www.citychicliving.com),* and began creating content for fashion, beauty, and lifestyle products, among other topic genres. The two businesses running harmoniously together exploded with success and the opportunities kept rolling in. I was offered a full paid scholarship to study for my Master's in Business at the University of

Memphis, featured in *Memphis Magazine's* Women Empowered issue, featured in the *Memphis Flyer's* top 20 under 30, flew out to Los Angeles to do celebrity makeup for a Grammy party and was featured on a slew of television news segments and editorial articles. Cutting loose from the security of my salaried job allowed me to pursue my passion. When we are truly passionate about what we do, naturally we shine and become noticed by others. Each and every one of these opportunities that came my way built upon each other to establish my brand and personal name as a professional in my industry, but more importantly, laid the foundation for the confidence I needed to succeed as an unconventional entrepreneur.

For another three years, I ran these two businesses parallel to one another, but in 2019 I faced a decision much like the one seven years prior. The digital creator business was almost as profitable as my store and could potentially surpass my shop profits if only I had the extra time. I'm sure you know what came next. I put my shop on the market and a buyer quickly came.

Since selling my business I have been working full-time as a digital entrepreneur on my blog and social platforms while consulting other aspiring entrepreneurs through my online school, The Unconventional Entrepreneur Academy. *(www.learnunconventional.com)*

As a digital entrepreneur, I spend my days creating content for many national brands to use in their digital strategies, as well as reviewing products and services from these brands on my social platforms. When I am not in photo shoots or planning my content calendar, I help other entrepreneurs streamline their business strategies and develop robust marketing plans. Through my journey as an entrepreneur, I have learned that my passion isn't really in one industry. My passion lies in the creation and launch of novel ideas, business design, and teaching others.

The first question I got when telling others that I was going back to school was, "Why? You have a successful business. Why do you need to go back to school?" The answer lies in my passion and nature as an unconventional entrepreneur. Despite what others may tell you, there is no "right path" to business success and with the evolution of technology, business strategies must continuously adapt to meet the ever-changing needs of the consumer. The synergy of innovative ideas, novel research, and knowledge gained from my experiences has motivated me to help cultivate this unconventional business culture into a societal norm so that we may all recognize and seize the opportunity to achieve our passion through work.

And there you have it, you are all caught up to the present day. Now, I know I threw a lot of ideas and background at you in this chapter, but let's get down to the nitty-gritty and the real reason you are here. What's in it for you? What is your unique, ornate skill set? One of the great wonders of life is your own personal wonder, the one thing that is eccentrically you. So, let's get to it! In Part 2, we will go over how to discover your skill set, because after all, we are all badass at something!

II
THE 8 ELEMENTS OF AN UNCONVENTIONAL ENTREPRENEUR

Learn about the 8 Elements of an Unconventional Entrepreneur, with special emphasis on determination, and take the questionnaire to assess your skill level within each element. Once you have a grasp of your strengths, the Discovery Kit will help you uncover your true passion and potential business opportunities. Every entrepreneur must know how to build and harness confidence to keep their wheels turning, so I will also give you my favorite confidence-boosting tips for ultimate success .

DISCOVER YOUR SKILL SET

Do you aspire to quit your job and become your own boss but have no clue what you want to do? Or maybe you have an idea of what you want to do but are unsure if you have the skill set to turn your dream into a successful business. While being an entrepreneur means freedom and flexibility in your work life it does require a multifaceted set of skills. It is important to understand which skills you currently excel with and which you could take a little time to brush up on. If you were to research the skills or traits of an entrepreneur, you would find a myriad of lists. While many sources list noteworthy entrepreneurial traits and skills, they differ in that they are all geared toward the traditional entrepreneur. In this chapter, I identify eight key elements that are essential for mastering the unconventional entrepreneur mindset. There really is no science behind these particular eight elements; however, in my experience, when you are tackling obstacles and planning for success in an evolving small business culture these eight elements are key when it comes to climbing to the top.

Before listing the eight key elements, I want to take a minute to address a question that is always asked. Do I already have these elements in my skill set, and if not, can I learn them? You notice I refer to both traits and skills in this chapter.

skill - 1: the ability to use one's knowledge effectively and readily in execution for performance, and 2: a learned power of doing something competently (Merriam-Webster Dictionary)

trait - 1: a distinguishing quality (as of personal character), and 2: an inherited characteristic. (Merriam-Webster Dictionary)

In analyzing the definition of *skill,* it is apparent that a skill is something that can be taught, learned, and therefore can be improved upon. However, research suggests that a trait is inherited but can be shaped by environmental factors. In any event, skills can be learned, and traits can evolve and be improved upon. In order to appreciate the properties of both skills and traits, I use the word *element* to reference the eight essential characteristics of an unconventional entrepreneur.

The 8 Elements of an Unconventional Entrepreneur

- Determination
- Adaptability
- Risk Taking
- Willingness to Learn
- Communication
- Assertiveness
- Problem Solving
- Creativity

Notice that "confidence" is not on the element list, but we will spend a lot of time talking about confidence, an entire chapter to be exact. Confidence is subjective and situational. Even those who view themselves as extremely confident may feel uncertainty and self-doubt when faced with an unfamiliar circumstance. The foundation of confidence is based on your current situation and perception of your own abilities. You can master each of the eight elements but still lack confidence; however, without confidence, your chances for success are greatly minimized. It is for this reason that we will dedicate an entire chapter to understanding and building your confidence.

The 8 Elements Personal Evaluation
Before we dive into the specifics of each element it is important to get an idea of where your strengths and weaknesses lie. This is not a scientifically proven scale. It is an evaluation I use with my clients to reveal top-line gaps in their skill set.

Scan the QR code to take the 8 Elements Questionnaire. Upon entering your email, you will receive an exclusive link to the questionnaire in your inbox. Answer all questions to the best of your ability; be honest with yourself. After answering the 25 questions, you will be able to tally up your score for each of the eight elements.

DEFINING THE 8 ELEMENTS

Determination

When the going gets tough, do you get going? Determination comes from an internal drive that motivates you to work hard and be committed to doing whatever it takes to reach your objectives. In this part of the book, you will learn how to effectively set goals and develop streamlined processes for achieving those goals. You need determination to navigate successfully through the daily twists and turns inherent in running a business. Without determination, it is near impossible to beat "time." Time is the sneaky culprit that will cause you to quit. Many entrepreneurs go through the "honeymoon phase" of launching their dream business but lose their determination a year or so into their project and abandon their dream altogether because of the time that is often needed to build success.

Determination will be the element that acts as the glue, holding you together in the toughest of times, when time itself seems to wear on your patience. A determined unconventional entrepreneur will put in the time needed to successfully complete the job, will avoid shortcuts, and will work meticulously to achieve their view of perfection.

Adaptability

Does sudden change throw you off course? In my opinion, adaptability is the second toughest of the eight elements, right behind risk-taking. It is so hard to take what life throws at you in the moment and make executive decisions at the same time, yet a master of adaptability does just that. The unconventional entrepreneur will experience bend and flex daily. Being able to creatively absorb changes and turn them into opportunities or push them out of your path based on what they can or cannot bring to the table, will help you to minimize stress and run a tight ship.

◆◆◆

Unconventional Wisdom

Always remain proactive. Building in time to act proactively in your business is more productive than falling victim to chasing chores reactively.

◆◆◆

Proper time management and prioritization will not only help you to stay focused among the interruptions but will enable you to take control of your time and schedule. So why is this essential to adaptability? Because prioritizing tasks in your planner while also allowing for flex time will keep your stress levels low; you will come to welcome flexibility in a more positive, opportunistic way. I block off three hours of my workday in the afternoon for unexpected meetings, outings, or even strategizing and brainstorming sudden opportunities. Such a practice will give you the flexibility to plan proactively for change instead of responding reactively to a situation.

Risk Taking

Do you welcome risk to benefit from the reward? As the old saying goes, "the greater the risk, the better the reward." On the flip side, the greater the risk, the greater the loss. One who scores high in the risk-taking element has the courage to act on great ideas without being deterred by risk, can make decisions blindly if needed, is comfortable with unfamiliar territory, and is willing to ride the waves to reach success. We don't always know what the outcomes of our decisions will be and are often faced with making decisions with minimal information and on intuition. This makes risk-taking the toughest of the eight elements. Starting a new business may feel like sailing uncharted waters with waves that can sink or buoy your ship. You are the captain. With each wave that crashes upon your bow, you will absorb the risk and seize that moment as an opportunity on your journey forward. Risk is just part of the game. If everyone could quit their job, start up a business, and become a millionaire, or in my case a thousand-aire, we wouldn't need books on the subject, everyone would have an enterprise, and the whole world would be rich. Doesn't that sound nice? One of the biggest elements that separate an unconventional entrepreneur from everyone else is their zest for facing risk. If you are absolutely unwilling to take risks, being a business owner is not the path for you.

◆ ◆ ◆

Unconventional Wisdom
One of the beauties of being an unconventional entrepreneur is the fluidity of structure, yet this fluidity often brings about uncertainty which makes way for new opportunity. And with every new opportunity, risk-taking is warranted to seize that moment.

◆ ◆ ◆

Risk-taking is very hard for many individuals. It is so much easier to stay with what you know than to flip life on its head and go after your dreams. But staying with what you know could possibly mean your untapped potential will lie dormant, never to be realized in your lifetime. To me, this translates to "regret at the end of the rope," if you know what I mean. Even the mere decision to pick up this book and peek over the fence at what opportunities may be available to you as an unconventional entrepreneur is a tiny risk. After facing this first risk, you may then decide to pursue the lifestyle of an unconventional entrepreneur and explore a world of flexibility, passion, and work-life balance.

Willingness to Learn

If you aspire to be an unconventional entrepreneur, it is important to understand that education and enrichment will be a lifelong process. A successful entrepreneur actively seeks new knowledge so that they may stay updated on trends that are happening within their market, on innovations that will allow them to expand into new markets, and on the competitive positions of other businesses. Furthering your education is not limited to journals and internet articles. An unconventional entrepreneur has an open mind to the personal advice and opinions of others. When I began my first business, I failed to network with fellow business owners in the retail industry. I had a concrete idea in my mind about how I was going to run a shop in an industry I had never worked in. Sounds pretty ridiculous, right? Indeed, it was. While in the end I figured out a winning strategy, I wasted months throwing spaghetti at the wall to see which noodles would stick. Narrow-mindedness is a detriment to growth. Building a network of experts in the field and being open to learning from both constructive criticism and unique ideas will boost your strategy to reach new heights.

◆◆◆

Unconventional Wisdom

Your business is a play and you are the puppet master. When you temporarily remove yourself from the plot and observe the landscape outside of the narrative, learning will ensue. This will enable you to clearly recognize new opportunities on the horizon and broaden your perspective.

◆◆◆

Communication

Have you ever had someone become less than pleasant about something you have unintentionally said or done? Paying attention to others' feelings, annoyances, and interests will help you to read the room and communicate in a mutually beneficial way. I made the mistake as a young entrepreneur of believing that my colleagues, because we worked so closely together, thought like I did, had the same viewpoints, and were motivated by the same things. I will be the first to raise my hand and say, "I was dreadfully wrong!" I can easily separate my personal life from my business activities, view criticism as an opportunity for improvement, and multitask like a MOTHER! I appreciate my family and peers "giving it to me straight," and therefore tend to be a straight shooter myself when it comes to communication.

In my early years of entrepreneurialism, I didn't know how to read non-verbal cues or body language well enough to see that my employees were not aligned with my communication style. My straight way of delivering messages sometimes came off as too direct. My tendency to divert conversation that was more personal and outside the scope of work came off as insensitive. And it turns out that "multitasking like a MOTHER" is not always the most effective way. I was jumping from one project to another, not giving thorough instructions, which left my employees confused and frustrated with the tasks I had assigned. I hate to admit this, but one of my employees complained to another that I was like the boss from "The Devil Wears Prada." Of course, I was a little shocked at the comment. My intentions were not to be a cold, hard "jerk" of a boss. I was only trying to manage twelve employees and run a super-tight ship so that I could hit my monthly sales goals, which would allow me to make payroll and satisfy other commitments I had made to my employees, customers, and family. My lack of communication skills blinded me to the perception of others and their needs. I did not take offense at the comparison, but instead, I quietly used the information as a personal opportunity for improvement. Communication is still an element that I actively work to improve. We may never be masters of every single element but being "willing to learn" will result in continuous improvements and help to cultivate meaningful partnerships.

Assertiveness

Do you get nervous when you are required to address a negative situation involving other people? Most people like to avoid confrontation at all costs, which unfortunately can muddy the waters on knowing when to take control of a situation or can lead to a "YES MAN" mentality.

yes man mentality - always saying "yes" when asked to do something, even when you do not have time to complete the task or even desire to do the task.

An assertive unconventional entrepreneur is a leader who will share their opinions on important topics and most importantly, know when to say no. Saying "yes" to everything that is put in front of you will uproot your strategy and your business will suffer. This was one of the hardest lessons for me to learn. As a budding entrepreneur, I said yes to every opportunity. I wanted to be helpful, worthy, and liked by those in my community. Eventually, I was performing tasks, speaking at events, and trading marketing services to the point that I had no time to focus on the activities that generated profits for my company. My bank account suffered, my company started to fall apart, and my spirits were broken. After desperate attempts to halt my business downfall, I began to ponder the causes of what seemed to be my impending demise. That was when it dawned on me, I had no flexibility because I said "yes" to everything that was asked of me. The day that I began to respectfully decline opportunities that I did not feel would benefit my business efforts was the day that I learned the power of assertiveness.

Problem Solving

Does the finality of making decisions cause you anxiety? This is one of the most talked about topics in my peer group. When a difficult problem arises, how do you solve the problem effectively? If you are unsure of the answer, do you just slap a Band-Aid on it? Someone who ranks higher in the problem-solving department redefines the problem before making a decision, observes the problem from every perspective, and seeks permanent solutions. When brushing up on my problem-solving skills, I realized that I often fell victim to the "experience trap." The experience trap is when you make decisions based on your past experiences. While learning from experience is great, not all problems have cookie-cutter solutions. You must be able to identify how the current problem and a previous obstacle are similar and different. Unfortunately, problem-solving is not an activity that should be undertaken with a quick trigger. In order to choose a solution that best fits the desired outcome, all elements should be observed. This does not mean that every problem has a complex solution. Many difficult problems can be adequately solved with simple solutions. While problem-solving sounds negative and most people will automatically feel negativity when they hear the word "problem," an unconventional entrepreneur understands that a problem is merely an opportunity for growth and excellence.

Creativity

Does your brain constantly dream up new and exciting ideas? I have been dreaming up different business ideas since I was a young girl. I used to make posters when I was six and sell them to members of my family. When I was eight, I started a neighborhood club in my parent's shed. We needed a whiteboard to go over our club goals and since my $5 allowance wouldn't cover it, I charged each club member $5 to join, which added up to the exact amount needed to purchase the whiteboard. When I was ten, I wrote a play and assigned all the children in my neighborhood club a part. My mom recalls being extremely surprised and somewhat mortified one Saturday afternoon when she answered the doorbell only to find a line of parents on our front porch coming to our house to see the play while handing over a $1 for their ticket. I got in a little bit of trouble for that one. I tried to explain that we needed the play proceeds for construction paper, glue sticks, and scissors for our club's craft activities. I knew she wouldn't go for a house full of strangers if I asked permission to host the play, so I decided to wing it. Creativity is an incredible element of the unconventional entrepreneur mindset. Being creative allows you to come up with fresh strategies and ways of doing business that will set you apart from your competition and help you to stand out. Many do not realize this, but creativity helps with problem-solving as well. Creatives are able to develop unique solutions to people's problems, which can lead to innovative products and services.

PERSONAL DEVELOPMENT ACTIVITIES

After the last section, you should have an idea of your ranking within the elements. I will now share some activities to help you further develop each element. I encourage you to grab a pen and paper, take a deep breath, and open your mind to these development activities and any new ideas that may come your way.

DETERMINATION

Activity Challenge

Try one new challenging activity per month. The goal is to overcome the challenge and push yourself outside of your comfort zone. Be sure that you cognitively block your mind from comparing yourself and your work to others. Healthfully benchmarking yourself is a positive practice; however, obsessively comparing your work can stifle your creativity. Remember, this is about overcoming with determination, which is best done by navigating the situation from your own perspective.

Research and list five challenging activities to further develop your determination element.

_____

_____

_____

_____

_____

ADAPTABILITY

Day Planning

For this one, you will need a planner. We spoke about committing to opportunities that encourage development and limiting activities that do not benefit your business or brand. Spend some time before you shut down for the day to plan the following day, hour by hour, in your planner.

Be sure to allot "flex time" so that when opportunities or obstacles arise you will have time to tackle them. If you do not end up using your flex time for unexpected opportunities or obstacles, use this precious time to brainstorm new business ideas.

I also like to include "easy win tasks" in my daily plan. These are small activities that do not take a lot of time to complete but make a positive difference in my company. This also allows me to check a few things off my to-do list. Nothing is more discouraging than a to-do list that lingers without one single objective met for the day. With easy-win tasks, you are sure to finish your day with accomplishments.

Assessment Training

When an opportunity suddenly presents itself, it is sometimes hard to determine right off the bat if the endeavor will be beneficial to your company. When the next opportunity arises, answer the following questions to assess the importance of the project and avoid the "Yes Man" mentality.

What is the opportunity?

_____

_____

What are the possible positive outcomes of this opportunity?

_____

_____

What are the possible negative outcomes of this opportunity?

_____

_____

What might be the long-term gain from this opportunity?

_____

_____

Will the gain benefit my business?

_____

_____

Do the positive outcomes outweigh the negative outcomes? Consider time, money, brand equity, customer value, innovation, etc. Oftentimes an immediate negative outcome is outweighed by a positive outcome because the long-term gain is greater than the immediate negative response. I recommend that you be very careful with your decision in this instance and always use your moral compass.

RISK-TAKING

Irrational Brainstorming

When you have a random, irrational thought that pops up in your head that feels exciting, motivational, and a little bit crazy, take the time to brainstorm those thoughts further. Some of my best ideas have come from weird and irrational thoughts that seemed risky at first, but when developed, transformed into a concept that worked! Accept your irrational thoughts!

What are some irrational business ideas and thoughts you have had lately?

_____

_____

_____

_____

_____

Avoid Dream Killers

Dream killers are those people in your life who are not risk takers, do not understand your passions, are not assertive, or really do not value any characteristics of an unconventional entrepreneur. You know who I am talking about. The people in your life who will be the first to tell you that quitting your job to pursue your dream is absurd. Those who instantly fuel you with fear of how you will be broke, will never make it, or will lose everything. I am not telling you to ditch family or lifelong friends, just refrain from discussing your work-life dreams with them. The dream killers will be the ones who hold you back and make you doubt yourself.

WILLINGNESS TO LEARN

Reading List
Subscribe to journals and blogs within your industry. Read a biography or autobiography of someone you admire in the business world. Knowledge is easy to find and often free. Research popular blogs, feeds, podcasts, social sites, and journals in your industry to create your reading/ listening list for continuous knowledge.

Your Reading/Listening List

_____

_____

_____

_____

_____

Observation For Learning
Turn failures into learning opportunities. Take the time to observe some of your biggest failures and consider how you would have done things differently if given the opportunity once again. This will give you wisdom and help you to develop your decision-making skills.

Think back to some of your biggest failures in life. What did you learn from them?

_____

_____

Could you have done something differently to produce a more positive outcome?

_____

_____

If you were to research a solution to the failure, what would you research?

_____

_____

Join Local Groups

Remember when we talked about keeping an open mind and learning from others in your field? Research local business clubs and social organizations. Your local Chamber of Commerce may have monthly get-togethers. Even community social events are great for networking.

Create a list of prospective groups to join.

_____

_____

_____

_____

_____

COMMUNICATION

Practice Listening and Eye Contact

Active listening will help you to further understand your peers. Likewise, eye contact will help you learn to recognize non-verbal cues. If you lack confidence, eye contact may feel uncomfortable. Practice natural eye contact while listening in parallel. After having an important conversation, write down three things that you learned and three non-verbal signs that you picked up on. This practice will tune your senses so that you may pick up verbal and non-verbal cues while communicating.

What did you learn?

_____

_____

What non-verbals did you pick up on?

_____

_____

"People Watch" for Non-Verbals

Find a high-traffic area, take a seat, and note the non-verbal cues you pick up from the people you observe. This is a great activity to do with a friend so that you can compare and discuss observations to help develop your open-mindedness.

What are their facial expressions?

_____

_____

How is their body posture?

_____

_____

Are they folding their arms when speaking?

_____

_____

Do they speak fluidly using their hands?

_____

_____

Plan Your Communication

Often, we plan a time for an important conversation, but we don't actually plan the conversation for success. Think about an upcoming conversation or meeting that you have planned and answer the following questions. Ask for honest feedback on how the meeting went. It is important to understand the perception and feelings of others to further develop your communication skills.

Will there be difficult topics?

_____

_____

Will the conversation cause excitement?

_____

_____

What are possible reactions to the message?

_____

_____

Once the conversation is over, record the outcome against your predictions.

Would you have done anything differently?

_____

_____

Did you learn something interesting about your colleague?

_____

_____

ASSERTIVENESS

Understand Comfort Levels

Some of us are assertive with specific activities and are passive with others. First, understand your comfort levels and then strategize for change.

Where are some areas in your life where you are assertive?

_____

_____

Give an example of times in which you are passive.

_____

_____

Evaluate where you are assertive in certain aspects and passive in others.

_____

_____

What can you do to turn some of the passive instances into assertive ones?

_____

_____

_____

_____

_____

_____

Cultivate an Assertive Attitude

In order to be respectfully assertive, you must develop trust within yourself and your leadership capabilities. Know your viewpoints and remove personal emotion from the equation so that you can achieve what is best for your brand, employees, customers, and overall morale.

In what areas do you lack when it comes to trusting yourself?

_____

_____

Observe the Reaction

When I started to be more assertive, it was really empowering for me. I expected the reaction of my peers to be a disappointment; however, the reaction was greater respect and understanding.

When you turned down a request, how did you do it and what was the reaction?

_____

_____

What are some ways that you can be respectfully assertive when turning down a request?

_____

_____

PROBLEM-SOLVING

Focus on the Root and the Whys

Oftentimes we jump to conclusions about what the actual problem is and fail to understand the root of the problem. For example, imagine that you are having problems getting to work on time. You think it is because you are trying to cram so many morning activities in before work which prevents you from leaving on time. But if you back it up and think deeper, you remember that you hit snooze on the alarm clock. This shortened the time you needed for your morning routine. Let's back it up a little more. Why did you hit snooze on the alarm clock? You remember that you didn't get to bed until 11 p.m. and you were too tired to get up when your alarm went off. Why didn't you go to bed until 11 p.m.? Because you watched your favorite reality show after the kids went to bed. Problem solver: No need to give up on the little personal indulgences; instead, record the reality show, choose some free time on the weekend to indulge, and stick to a set bedtime. The problem was not a busy morning routine, it was that you watched the reality show, which caused you to stay up too late, which meant that you did not get enough sleep, which then caused a snowball effect on the rest of your plans for the following day. This is a super-simple example, but if you focus on the root and the whys of complex problems, you may be surprised to learn the real issue at hand.

What is a problem you have been facing lately?

_____

_____

Ask yourself WHY until you get to the root of the problem. What are your WHYS?

_____

_____

What is/are the solution(s)?

_____

_____

Think Laterally

When thinking laterally, your approach to problem-solving is generally indirect and more creative. We tend to dig to find solutions that are directly linked to our problems. Try thinking about the issue at hand and consider solutions that may not be directly linked to the problem. Instead of thinking about the activities that happened before or after the problem, think about the environment that surrounds the problem. Thinking laterally helps to cultivate innovative solutions.

CREATIVITY

Allocate a Creative Space

Change up your surroundings to evoke inspiration. Choose a space in your home to allocate as your "creative space." Fill this space with inspirational reads, images, posters, art, etc. Nothing sucks the life out of creativity worse than a drab, dark workspace. Make going to work fun and inspirational.

Idea Book

Carry a dedicated idea notebook with you so that you can jot down ideas in real-time. Unconventional entrepreneurs have ideas that fly in and out of their heads at unexpected times since inspiration can be sparked in an instant. Be sure to capture those ideas. Some of my greatest business ideas have come to me at random times. When I don't write them down, I almost always forget them. Writing down my ideas not only helps me to remember but allows me to review my thoughts in conjunction with others. Reviewing my ideas with others can spark even more innovative thoughts.

Tap into the Senses

Physical acts, especially those that tap into the senses, help to shape innovative thoughts. Creative projects that play on more than one of your senses can help to activate an enhanced creative consciousness. A pottery class uses your hands, sight, and smell. As I write this chapter, I am listening to classical music, typing with my hands, and thoughtfully crafting my words so that they may easily transmit from this book to your brain. Try a class that requires you to use more than one of your senses. You will be amazed at the way your brain creatively activates for enhanced thinking and novel ideas.

Before moving into a deep dive on determination and confidence, I would like to share with you an extensive process for discovering your hard skill. The eight elements we just reviewed are soft skills that can evolve over time with experience and growth activities. Your "gift(s)" is a hard skill that can be further developed into a profitable business. You may have an idea of what your gift(s) is. The following activity in the next chapter will help you to expand further in your assessment and even possibly reveal a portfolio of gifts that can build upon one another.

THE WORK-LIFE DREAM DISCOVERY KIT

What is it that moves you? Dig deep. We all have a gift or skill that we secretly admire about ourselves, one that we have carried through life. A "feel in your bones" kind of situation. Maybe this gift is a current hobby? Maybe it is something that you loved to do as a child? I always say that those things that inspired us as innocent, young children often hold the key to our passion as an adult. Being an unconventional entrepreneur is unique in that, once you have cultivated a business that is focused on your passion, you begin to enjoy life on a deeper level and have an appreciation for the little things that you never really noticed before. As an unconventional entrepreneur, I feel like my zest for life has evolved to a completely different plane. Hypothetically speaking, taste is richer, colors are more vivid, and the air is sweeter. I have much more gratitude. You can really breathe in all the possibilities of life when you are living in your passion. So here it is, time to reveal your gift, your hard skill, the one thing that you can turn into your work-life dream!

Scan the QR code and enter your email to receive the Discovery Kit in your inbox. Before completing these worksheets, read below to better understand the Peer Interview Questionnaire and Self-Evaluation Worksheet activities.

Scan the Code

Peer Evaluation Questionnaires

Many of us have an idea of what our gift is but need further discovery to develop it into a business idea. Others are quite the opposite. Some are called to build their work-life dream but have not identified their hard skill. Before brainstorming your business ideas too deeply, scan the code above, print the Discovery Packet that will be emailed to you, and set up individual interviews with three people who are closest to you. You will use the Peer Interview Questionnaire to conduct these interviews. Sometimes, others recognize our gifts, even if we are blind to them. The reason you should not zoom in on your business ideas at this point is because you need to remain open to the possibilities and manifestations that this activity will provide. Once you have interviewed all three people, combine their answers and brainstorm new possibilities.

Self-Evaluation Worksheet

Now, it is time to get real with yourself. Find a space where you can be alone, unbothered, and inspired. Classical music and a candle always help to clear my brain and set the mood so that I can think creatively. I want you to consider what you have learned from your peer evaluations and answer the questions on the Self-Evaluation Worksheet truthfully and with an inventive mindset. It is important to take your time on each question so that your ideas and thoughts will flow freely. After this activity, you should begin to be a little more in touch with your passion and business idea.

Notes:

_____
_____
_____
_____
_____
_____
_____
_____
_____
_____

DETERMINATION IS KEY

Before diving in, I feel it is very important that we take a moment to chew on the definitions of determined.

determined - 1: having a strong feeling that you are going to do something and that you will not allow anyone or anything to stop you, and 2: not weak or uncertain.
(Britannica Dictionary)

There are three action items that make up this definition: have strong feeling, do something, not allow. Developing a strong feeling is the fun part, doing something about that feeling is the hard part, and not allowing anyone to stand in your way is the effortless part.

In my experience, *having a strong feeling* is the fun and creative part of cultivating determination. A *strong feeling* amounts to our personal, unyielding attitude about something, in this instance, your work-life passion. If you have picked up this book, I can guarantee that you have already achieved the first action item of determination. If you did not have a strong feeling within you about becoming an unconventional entrepreneur or changing your working lifestyle, you wouldn't have been motivated to read more about the topic. So congratulations, you are one step closer to achieving true determination.

Oftentimes, especially with creatives like myself, innovative ideas start out as a strong feeling and then they hit a wall. Dreaming up the most amazing business ideas, processes, products, services, and brands is absolutely exhilarating. I tend to go down a rabbit hole, spouting off one idea after another until I feel strongly about a particular project, but become stagnate when it comes to taking action, or *doing something*. This book for example. This has been a project on my to-do list for more than five years. I have written outline after outline on what my book would entail but always let the project get stale. You might call this laziness or could say that I had too much on my plate, but I know that neither is the case. Not following through on my strong desire to help others achieve work-life freedom and the unconventional entrepreneurial dream was due to my lack of confidence. Being fully transparent about my experiences and deep personal ideas on how business has evolved and should now be practiced seemed like a valuable contribution to the small business world. At the same time, the uncertainty of how my peers would review my efforts held me back. It was the fear of what others might think and a lack of confidence that inhibited me from taking action or *doing something*.

Action item 2 in the definition of determination is to *do something*. This is the biggest and hardest step for most people. There are many things that may prevent you from taking action on your *strong feeling*, but in most cases, lack of knowledge or confidence are the culprits. As you can see from my experience, in the past, lack of confidence played a huge role in holding me back. That's why I feel it is necessary to include a chapter on confidence in this book. Actually taking the first step may mean that you have to be willing to reroute your current life path, trust in yourself, or take risks, which all can be very scary.

Only you can choose to achieve your true potential. Facing the unknown means obstacles, ups, downs, and learning curves but I promise you, the rewards are worth it. I don't just mean material rewards. Through this journey, I have learned so much about myself. I have met a woman within that I never knew existed and I can say with complete humility that I am extremely proud of who she is and what she has accomplished. I would have never viewed myself in this light or trusted in my abilities had I not chosen to *do something*. This self-realization had such a profound impact on my life. I truly believe that I would have led a life unfulfilled had I not chosen to *do something* about this unconventional dream of mine. This borderline, out-of-body journey is one that everyone with the same aspiration must experience to attain that piece of fulfillment that might otherwise never be realized.

◆ ◆ ◆

Unconventional Wisdom
You only have one life to live. You can choose to carry on in mediocrity or go bravely into the unknown and seize all that life has to offer.

◆ ◆ ◆

Things have gotten heavy in here! Let's move on to the easy part. Once you have taken action on your strong ideas, you have no other option than to get the job done! This means that you will <u>not allow</u> anyone to stand in your way. This is quite effortless once you have officially set out on your path. This doesn't mean you'll ignore your peers, family, or support groups. Considering the ideas, constructive criticisms, and guidance of others who have embarked on a similar journey will prove to be very beneficial. As we discussed before, avoid the dream killers so that you may set forth and conquer success!

Cultivating Determination

Feeling determined yet? Remember that determination is one of the eight elements of an unconventional entrepreneur. Each action item in the definition of determination will help you to banish weakness and uncertainty. Answer the following questions truthfully so that you may improve upon the element of determination and better align yourself for success as an unconventional entrepreneur.

What is your <u>strong feeling</u>? Your creative idea?

_____

_____

What is holding you back from taking the first step? List everything that comes to mind.

_____

_____

What will you <u>do</u> about these obstacles and how will you <u>not</u> <u>allow</u> defeat?

_____

_____

THE CONFIDENCE LOOP

As Taylor Swift once, or a thousand times, said, "Haters gonna hate, hate, hate, hate, hate." Words spoken from a true boss babe! Believe me, I have certainly had my fair share of haters. In honor of my husband's girl crush, Taylor Swift, in this chapter, we are going to banish the haters and overcome with a colossal amount of confidence.

"Thank you so much to absolutely everyone who had a negative thing to say about me, disliked me, or bullied me. Because of you, I have learned to look at life more deeply and have experienced the liberation of marching to the beat of my own drum. There is nothing sweeter than being able to be unapologetically me and I thank you for giving me the fuel to discover the power of confidence."

Although my shout-out seems a little salty, it truly isn't. I genuinely mean it with complete sincerity. Want to know a little secret? I haven't always had confidence, and even now at times, my confidence can waver.

As a young child, I didn't worry much about what others thought. I was blessed that I grew up in an environment where I would always hear the adults in my life talk about how I possessed leadership-type qualities, and how I was going to do big things. It made me feel proud of myself. Surely, they were biased. After all, those adults were my parents. I can't remember a time as a young child when I actually doubted myself. I guess that is the beauty of innocence. As children we explore self-interests, are void of responsibilities, and for many of us, really have nothing other than eat, sleep, and play on the agenda. Remember those days?

As I reached adolescence, I began to focus my attention outwards and became very cognitive of others' opinions. This is normal development, as it is the natural progression from childhood into becoming an adult, yet at this social exploration phase in our lives, our confidence is on the line. "Other's opinions" are the ultimate confidence killers! At the adolescence stage, we first begin to question what others think about us and our actions, our self-trust begins to crack, and fear can easily set in.

In my adolescence, I detected two types of mindsets that really stood out. There were the "opinionated," those who are seemingly judgmental and tend to criticize others, and then there are the "sensitives," those who are people-pleasers and sensitive to the thoughts and feelings of their peers. At first glance, one could assume that the opinionated would be driven down the path of leadership, while sensitives would be driven towards a discipleship journey. However, we cannot draw an assumption of who will become leaders versus those who will become followers based on these mindsets alone.

There seems to be one common driver that prevents either mindset from achieving leadership status. Interestingly enough, both groups are often driven by the same thing, fear. And because the fears that emerge during our adolescence have a tendency to follow us into adulthood, it is easy for one to remain in these limiting mindsets even as we grow older. For many of us, our reaction to fear is a revolving, self-destructive process. When an "opinionated" becomes fearful or experiences a social setting in which they feel threat, they tend to outwardly criticize and become judgmental. On the other hand, when the "sensitive" becomes fearful or experiences a social setting in which they feel threat, they tend to dwell on the opinions of others and go out of their way to fix the situation, which can cause further destruction. It is fear that causes us to experience levels of anxiety and it is anxiety that feeds mistrust in ourselves, which can stifle leadership development.

When I reached adolescence, a sensitive mindset began to emerge. I actually remember the specific incident that seemed to be the turning point. The truth is, I was pretty oblivious to others' opinions of me until the age of ten when I began to get bullied. I moved to a new school in a different state, and it quickly became apparent that I didn't fit in. There were people who didn't like me, and I struggled deeply with that. I couldn't understand at the time what was going on. At my old school, I was the girl that moved between cliques effortlessly, not really tied down to any particular group, but easily making lasting friends all around. This dynamic seemed to work out for me, so when it came time to move schools, I had 100% confidence, without a fear in the world, that I was going to pop right in and never miss a beat. I was terribly wrong. I instantly became an outcast. I was constantly bullied, had few friends, and often cried quietly in my room. Because I was a sensitive, I tried to make the best of it and didn't fill my parents in on what was going on until later. Even worse, because I was a sensitive, being the butt of all the jokes really took a toll on me. I can now see that at the time I experienced a change in how I saw myself.

For the first time in my life, I was scared and lacked major confidence. I hated it. I missed the old me, the little girl who was so creative and innovative and couldn't care less about the opinions of others. It was a never-ending circle. I would get bullied, I would dwell on what I must be doing wrong, and then, because I have always been determined as hell, I would go back to school the next day with a plan to make the bullies like me. Guess what? It never worked. The reason was that the bullies were picking on me out of fear. What did they have to be fearful of? At the age of ten, I was in my first year of middle school, sixth grade, which is a pretty anxious time for all. Being in sixth grade, regardless of gender, you are the "fresh meat" of the school. You hear all these stories of older, eighth-grade kids hazing the new students. Middle school can be the ultimate power struggle, with your hierarchical status depending upon your friend group. Therefore, the bullies needed to maintain status to exist in the eyes of others. Their fear and anxiety of ending up in my boat fueled their actions against me and others like me. This is just one example. I could go on and on but I will save my "unconventional school years" for another book.

Want to know how I overcame and succeeded with my first life lesson in confidence? I had it ingrained in my head, "never become the victim." To me, it doesn't really mean what it reads. For me personally, it meant that I wasn't going to feel like a victim or let anyone know that they were actually victimizing me. Instead, I picked up my head and did the only other thing I knew how to do at ten years old. I RAN. I ended up changing schools at the end of my sixth-grade year in hopes that I would never see those kids again. A typical reaction of an eleven-year-old; however, running away is definitely not the reaction that I would recommend. Sooner or later, you will be forced to square off with your demons, whether they be sixth-grade assholes or a more substantial issue such as a lack of trust in yourself.

Running only prolonged the issue that was inevitable. What I hadn't taken into account was that all of the middle school students would be going to the same high school, so I would once again come face-to-face with the same situation as in sixth grade. The anxiety and fear as I finished my eighth-grade year were unreal. I couldn't bear the thought that I would possibly be spending the next four years of my life in high school being bullied.

The summer before starting ninth grade I was fourteen years old and a little more developed in my mindset. I made the cognitive decision to stay true to myself, be kind to others no matter what, stand strong through the face of adversity, and stick to my tactic of being a part of many worlds, of many social groups, not being exclusive to any one group, but having friends from all circles. I also told myself that I wasn't going to chase friends or spend copious amounts of time trying to make people like me. While the sensitive mindset has its moments, creeping back up in my adulthood, that year was the first time I acknowledged and broke free from that destructive pattern.

◆ ◆ ◆

Unconventional Wisdom
Exist in many worlds.

◆ ◆ ◆

What happened when school started? I saw almost all of those people who had made my life hell in middle school. I was relieved that not one of them even remembered me. Actually, I became friends with two of them in high school and asked both of them at some point during high school if they remembered me in middle school. When they both replied, "You went to middle school with us?" I never brought it up again. To this day, I have never mentioned how they destroyed six months of my life. What's the point? I don't let the sensitive mindset control me anymore so there really is no room for dwelling, and they turned out to be pretty great people. Seems like they too broke free of their destructive, opinionated patterns. After all, in the end, it was middle school, and we were all trying to survive.

Oh, if life could be only as hard as middle school, right? Although life has gotten more complicated as I have grown older, living with confidence has made it a piece of cake, and an enjoyable piece of cake at that. It is confidence that levels the playing field. Confidence enables you to set fear aside and take the actions needed to achieve success.

confidence - the state of feeling confident about the <u>truth</u> of something; a feeling of <u>self-assurance</u> arising from one's appreciation of <u>one's own abilities</u> or qualities. (Oxford Lexico)

In looking at the definition, per Oxford Languages, confidence really boils down to three components, *trust*, *action*, and *appreciation*. Feeling confident in the "truth" of yourself is having trust in yourself. One's abilities would imply action, as there must be some sort of action taking place to realize your abilities. And while some would say that it is pompous to be so sure of yourself, I would argue that self-assurance garners self-appreciation which is essential for achieving higher levels of confidence. Each feeds off of one another in a never-ending loop that I call, The Confidence Loop. Trusting in yourself feeds into taking action, which feeds into self-assurance, which feeds into confidence, which then feeds into greater trust in yourself. And so, the loop continues.

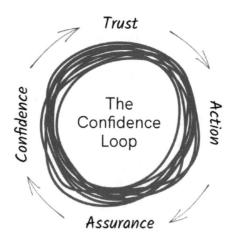

I have experienced this circular process first-hand on numerous occasions. One notable experience was quitting my job in 2012. Quitting my job meant that there was some level of trust in myself, but I can assure you it was just enough to push me to take action. After taking the first step and actively making my dream of owning a business come true, I looked at myself differently. I couldn't believe that the tiny bit of trust I had placed in myself ended up being a fruitful business. Having a little faith in my abilities taught me a lot about myself. It was like meeting a woman within that I never knew existed, and I quite liked her. She put her skills to the test, created a brand from scratch, and launched a successful business.

While there was still much to learn about business, from this experience my confidence grew in the areas of branding and launching. Because my confidence grew, when it came time to expand to a second location, I had greater trust in myself and it was easier for me to take action. Once I successfully launched my second boutique, I had greater self-assurance in my knowledge of financial strategy and inventory management. Of course, there is always still more to learn, and so the loop goes on. Once you have traveled the loop a handful of times, your confidence, trust, and assurance will become so solid that you will quit second-guessing yourself and instead will quickly take action when an opportunity arises.

Now that we know more about the basis of confidence, I am going to share three tactics that I use when it comes to boosting and keeping confidence.

- Live in Many Circles
- Adjust Your Vocabulary
- Manifest Confidence

Live in Many Circles
In my childhood story, I mentioned that I positioned myself in many social groups, in many circles. This is a tactic that I have continued to use in my unconventional entrepreneurial lifestyle. I am involved in many different organizations within my community and network with all different types of professionals, big and small. I don't box myself into one group or market. How does this promote confidence? When you don't box yourself in, you aren't as invested or influenced by the personal opinions or thoughts of a small group of people. I am not saying that these opinions or thoughts are not of value. I have learned invaluable lessons from the most unexpected interactions and from

professionals who aren't even in my field. However, when you restrict your circle to just one or two groups business can become personal and the opinions of a narrow slice of the world can damper confidence. Many may say that this is the act of building a wall, I call it like it is and say that this is the act of protecting one of your most valuable assets, confidence. When it comes to home life, I am very affected by the opinions of my family and close friends, but in terms of business, my goals are my focus, and confidence is needed to achieve those goals, therefore, I guard my confidence closely.

Adjust Your Vocabulary

When I quit my corporate job, people continuously asked, "What if you fail?" The only response that I had was, "I have removed failure from my vocabulary." Seems smug, but it has become a mantra that I use today when my confidence starts to waver. This doesn't mean that I haven't had small failures along the way. Sure, I've had major ups and downs as I have navigated my way through different business environments, but when I hit those lows and begin to feel a tinge of defeat, I remind myself, "Failure is not in my vocabulary." Because it is not in my vocabulary, when I start to think that maybe I have failed, my brain is conditioned to drop the thought and take action. I pop back up, get back to the drawing board as quickly as possible, remind myself of previous successes, and trust in myself to get back on the path as I have done so many times before. What word negatively triggers you? Adjust your vocabulary to eliminate that trigger. Turn that word into a powerful mantra that not only pulls confidence to the forefront but triggers action and reminds you of the trust and assurance that you have in yourself.

◆ ◆ ◆

Unconventional Wisdom
Remove failure from your mindset.

◆ ◆ ◆

Manifest Confidence

It may sound silly. I must admit, I am not an expert in this field. I know there are tons of amazing books on the power of manifestation and while I have not written down my wishes over and over to manifest them into reality, that's not the point. I interpret manifestation like I do most things, via the dictionary.

manifest - to make evident or certain by showing or displaying.
  (Merriam Webster)

The more you exude confidence in social settings, the more you will manifest confidence within yourself. This is how it works. Whether you feel completely confident or not, if you project confidence into the world, others will view you as confident, will develop respect for you, and in return, you will build confidence within yourself. Have you ever met that person who may not be the smartest, best looking, richest, tallest (the list goes on) person? The person whose outward appearance doesn't match what society deems "perfect" but they seem to draw people to them like a magnet every time they enter the room? The "opinionated mindset" would automatically think to themselves, "What does she have that I don't? Why does everyone seem to love her? She's not good-looking. She's not tall. She's not fit. She doesn't have money." Do you know why everyone loves her? Because she is confident. She humbly loves herself. She isn't bothered by the opinions of the opinionated. She manifests confidence which demands respect and wins the hearts of her colleagues. Because of this, people want to be around her. Her confidence has transformed her into a leader. Of course, a leader is much more than just confidence, but confidence is the first step. Humble confidence is the foundation to building a following and strong bones for becoming a leader.

Understand why I dedicated an entire chapter on the subject? Confidence is everything when it comes to being an unconventional entrepreneur. If you have the utmost confidence in yourself, you will not be held back by "fear of the unknown," which creeps up when launching a business. You will not be held back by the "dream killers" who tell you that you shouldn't follow this path. Nothing will keep you from pursuing your passion because your self-trust and appreciation will carry you through.

Notes:

_____
_____
_____
_____
_____
_____
_____
_____
_____
_____

III
THE UNCONVENTIONAL
BRAND STRATEGY

My favorite part of the business development process is giving identity to my ideas. There is something about packaging ideas into a tangible brand that breathes life and purpose into the project. A business idea without a brand is merely an abstraction floating around in the ethos that could potentially be your future career, but once you solidify your brand name, look, and voice, your idea is pulled from the mind and made whole in the material world.

HUMANIZING YOUR BRAND

One of the first times in history that we see branding being used for modern business practices was during the fifteenth century when ranch owners would burn a personal identifying mark on their cattle to show ownership. As business began to reshape over time, the idea of branding began to evolve with it. With the nineteenth-century rise of trade and mass production, businesses began putting their mark on packaging not only for identity but also to represent quality. During this time period, the idea of branding began to evolve from an identifying mark of ownership to a mark representing product caliber. In the twentieth century, marketing mediums such as radio and TV were used to broadcast their nifty product name, color schemes, jingles, and benefits in an effort to persuade consumers to purchase. Companies strategized against their competition through the development of superior products and top-notch services, which in turn, built brand identity and equity. This "top-down" approach has worked magnificently over the past 150 years. However, due to the extreme technological, market, and consumer preference changes over the past several decades, the top-down strategy is no longer a viable one.

More than ever, consumers are playing an active role in shaping and defining brands *(Campbell and Price, 2021)* because they use these brands to signal and communicate aspects of their own identity with their peers *(Berger and Heath, 2007)*. The evolution of brand purpose started with *ownership*, moved into *business quality representation*, and has now taken an emotional jump over to *consumer identity*. Because of this, unconventional entrepreneurs must focus on a consumer-driven approach, developing their brand through the eyes of their target market while also remaining unique and distinctive in their business culture.

My favorite part of the business development process is giving identity to my ideas. There is something about packaging ideas into a tangible brand that breathes life and purpose into the project. A business idea without a brand is merely an abstraction floating around in the ethos that could potentially be your future career. Many aspiring entrepreneurs have a laundry list of ideas but these ideas, unfortunately, remain on the "dream plane." You know, the place in our mind that we always go to when trying to escape the reality of our "less than ideal" work life?

dream plane - a level of existence or thought separate from the real world.

The dream plane, for most of us, is a coping mechanism, giving us hope and an ideal existence absent apart from the physical world. Drifting off into deep thought with a rumination about achieving financial stability, work-life flexibility, freedom of choice, exercising my knowledge, or taking control of my life, kept me motivated about my future, but it seemed these thoughts would never escape the dream plane. One day, while daydreaming, I was jolted from my musings with an obvious yet previously unthought-of idea. I had an epiphany. I didn't have to live somewhere in between my parallel lives of dreams and reality. I could merge my internal and external existence into reality and start living the work-life dream. It is a simple yet deep concept when you think about it. Just as an artist paints a canvas or an author writes a book, so does the entrepreneur brand a concept, but we must get out of our heads to do so. Art can be imagined but doesn't become art until it is created in the physical world for all to admire.

◆ ◆ ◆

Unconventional Wisdom
The moment you take an idea from the internal brain and execute it in the external world, it exists outside of you and reaches a level of tangibility.

◆ ◆ ◆

Branding is art and like any piece of art, its value is in the eyes of the beholder. So how do we create value in our brand strategy? Due to rising consumer demand to emotionally connect with products and services and the wide array of competition vying to be the first to meet the needs of the market, the unconventional entrepreneur must *humanize their brand for emotional satisfaction* while also *striving to appeal to the consumer.* These two aspects of branding will help to establish higher value in the eyes of the beholder.

Humanizing a brand means to engage your clients by educating them and connecting with them versus the age-old strategy of purely selling to them. This authentic connection allows you to be relatable to your market, builds trust, and satisfies the consumer's need for an emotional connection with the brand. It makes perfect sense when you think about it. Are you more likely to emotionally connect with an object or a person? Most of us are more likely to connect with a fellow human and since consumers desire this emotional connection with brands, an unconventional entrepreneur will devise a strategy to humanize their brand.

Adding a human aspect to my brand was one of the biggest obstacles that I overcame in my first business. After years of growing my makeup services business, I decided to expand my brand into a product line. I chose a name with no real meaning, but one in which I thought evoked beauty and femininity. The packaging was a beautiful shiny black with my light pink logo printed elegantly on the compact, and the key selling point seemed as attractive as the look of my product.

Key Selling Point
This cosmetic line will correct your skin while you wear it. We wear makeup all day long, so why not use a product that will benefit and improve your complexion?

My young entrepreneur mindset led me to believe that this was the perfect brand strategy for instant success. While I did sell quite a bit after launching the line, sales were not at the level I needed to make a full-time income from my efforts. It was clear that I didn't understand the assignment. I had been an established makeup artist, working many designer cosmetic events, featured in several publications, and booked solid with weddings, editorial shoots, and even a few celebrity events. It was a huge miss not to brand my expertise as an artist, but to instead launch a brand absent my accomplishments with merely a great motto and pretty packaging. After a few years of putting my all into this business, I hit a wall. Sales were flat, yet I was working major overtime to take my business to the next level. I needed a new game plan, a plan to merge my service and product offerings, as well as to humanize the brand.

I had connected with so many people through the service aspect of the industry and built a regional name as a makeup artist, but I was not using these achievements to back my brand. The rebranding strategy of my cosmetic line involved putting myself at the forefront by using my professional status in the cosmetic industry and evolving my marketing messaging beyond product features. The rebrand position assured customers that they could rely on a trusted and experienced expert who has developed a makeup line based on her clients' needs, which she had observed over many years in the industry. Choosing my cosmetic line meant that you would get an expert behind the brand. This rebrand allowed me to kill two birds with one stone: a human to facilitate an emotional connection and an expert to help the customer with their needs. The brand evolved into one that educated and provided added value versus one that existed to be sold.

People do not want to be sold to and often shut down immediately at any sign of a sales pitch. Instead, people seek solutions to their problems. The minute I stopped pushing a sales strategy and started to ask questions about what my clients needed in an effort to build a relationship and find a targeted solution, I was not only able to empathize with and understand my client's specific problems, but I also began connecting with them on a personal level. My clients appreciated the expertise and experience they received from my brand rather than a basic sales pitch that simply blended in with my competition.

Another interesting example outside of branding, but with the same goal of connecting with a product, was my own desire to understand a piece of art in my home. I discovered the piece of art in a beautiful bed and breakfast on a weekend getaway. I enjoyed my time at The Reserve Bed and Breakfast so much that I went online and purchased a recreation of the oil painting that was on display in our guest room. I hung this art in our room at home so that I could have my own personal piece of The Reserve Bed and Breakfast to remind me of our wonderful time. My interest in the painting motivated me to research more about the woman in the painting and the artist behind the piece. I learned that John Singer Sargent's famous portrait of Madame X painting was quite the scandalous topic of its time and when put on display at Paris Salon in 1884, it garnered a very controversial reception. I immediately connected with the story and began to treasure and admire the piece even more. When it was time to find a piece of art for our living room, I instantly researched more John Singer Sargent works. I fell in love with and purchased another John Singer Sargent piece called Elizabeth Winthrop Chanler. Of course, as with Madame X, I researched the painting and discovered that there is a lot on the internet about the model, Elizabeth Winthrop Chanler or "Bessie," and her extravagant life as an American heiress during the Gilded Age. Her childhood home has been listed on the historical registry and is open in Barrytown, New York, as a museum today. Because of my desire to further connect with the artist and the woman in the painting, I have added Barrytown to my bucket list of trips. While this is not an example of an emotional connection directly to a brand, this does mimic the human desire to connect with items on a more personal level. This is the power behind humanizing your brand.

By now, you should have a product or service in mind. Before getting deep into the brand development process of color schemes, names, etcetera, first brainstorm ways to humanize your brand. This will give you an idea of how you want to position your offering, which will also facilitate your physical vision.

Give Your Brand Personality

If your product or service had a voice, what would it sound like? Would it be quirky, organic, professional, humorous, playful, aggressive, neighborly, or luxurious? This voice is called "brand tone." Brand tone gives your brand a sense of personality. Think about the Old Spice brand. Their comical commercials and quick-witted text on the internet gives their brand a humorous personality that their audience enjoys and can relate to. This humorous personality draws their target market in and helps to establish an emotional connection between Old Spice and its customers.

Establishing the brand tone upfront will allow you to better align your brand's overall look and feel to help complete the total brand package. Did you know there are studies about the relationship between colors and emotions? Even type fonts can provoke a reaction from the reader. Once you establish your brand personality, you can better decide upon the physical aspects (logo, font, color scheme, etc.) that will constitute your brand.

Market Expert

Work to establish yourself as an expert in your market. Once consumers trust and bond with you as a professional, they are more likely to emotionally connect to your products and services. If you are not yet at expert level in your craft, invest in yourself. There are many accredited online courses that are industry-specific. Research to see if there is a well-known expert in your industry who offers online classes.

While not always industry-specific, the U.S. government offers a list of small business development centers through the Small Business Administration (SBA) website. (*sba.gov*) Networking with these groups can help you make connections with others in your local business community who may know business professionals in your specific market. If you already have expert credentials, include a PR strategy in your brand launch that introduces you as a pro. Reach out to local news stations, magazines, websites, blogs, podcasts, and social platforms to offer your professional advice. Remember, educate, DON'T SELL. Once your market recognizes and trusts that you are the expert, they will naturally gravitate towards your products to meet their solutions.

From Product to Experience

Create touch points and events so that your audience may connect with you personally. The most obvious touch point would be social media. This is the perfect medium for introducing your brand personality and tone, as well as yourself, to your target market. Another touch point would be to create a behind-the-scenes experience where you can personally meet your audience. For example, vineyards conduct winery tours, bath and body brands host soap making shops, or clothing stores set up personal styling sessions at events. Consider ways for your customer to experience your brand on a deeper, more interactive, level.

4 SENSES STRATEGY

Once you have an idea of how you will humanize your brand, you are ready to create its tangible aspects, such as brand name, color schemes, logos, fonts, and your overall brand identity. The unconventional entrepreneur uses a brand development process that works to excite the senses and cultivates a cohesive brand.

What do we know about the senses? We use five basic human senses to experience our environment and that sensory input creates our perceptions about the world in which we live. Likewise, the sensory input derived from touch, sight, sound, and smell is crucial to a brand development strategy. While taste is a very important sense, I do not include taste in my 4 Senses Branding Strategy as it is related specifically to something that can be consumed and is not generalizable across all markets. When developing your brand and its attributes, you must use what we know about the senses to ensure that your brand is relatable and truly captures the heart of your target market.

◆ ◆ ◆

Unconventional Wisdom
Become a brand that excites the senses.

◆ ◆ ◆

Sound

Believe it or not, the sound of my brand was the first vision I had of my business, even before choosing a color scheme, font, or business name. You may be wondering how this could be true when I was trying to brand a retail store and not an orchestra. Have you ever heard the phrase, "music speaks?" I tend to get very moved by different music genres and can easily be transported into a place in my head that allows me to explore emotions, feelings, and even creative ideas when listening to specific tunes. In my early 20s, I was like any typical young woman in that I loved the Top 100s in music and jammed to the newest beats when out having fun with friends. However, behind closed doors, when I was playing around in my closet, accessorizing and matching different fashion pieces while enjoying a bottle, I mean a glass, of wine, I would always put on Frank Sinatra and get lost in the nostalgia of what I imagined the Golden Age to be like. Living alone can be lonely at times, yet these moments became so special and treasured as I look back and remember a time of growth and self-assurance. It was during this period that I developed enough confidence to venture into the world of entrepreneurialism.

In the early stages of branding my boutique, before I had a brand name, color scheme, logo, or any real brand concept, I had this idea that I would play jazzy music for an upbeat, yet classy vibe. I wanted to induce the same classy, lavish, empowering feeling for my customers that I had those nights when messing around in my closet, styling my wardrobe, and playing in my makeup. I wanted my brand to invoke the idea that you don't have to be a rich girl to feel like a rich girl. This unconventional strategy of first imagining the sound of my brand really helped to put my brain in gear for business brainstorming. As I said, I did not have my brand name decided upon at this point. The brand name was actually the last aspect I solidified of the brand. I ended up calling my store The Ivory Closet to pay homage to my nights trying new makeup looks and wardrobe styling in my apartment closet while singing to Ol' Blue Eyes. And you guessed it, when I finally launched my first shop, I played jazzy music and even offered a sampling of wine for my customers to enjoy while shopping. Speaking of my brand name, notice how I included an aspect of color?

Sight

Because aspects of sight, such as color, are directly linked to emotion, sight is one of the most important senses in brand strategy. Studies have found that in all age groups, "colors and emotions are consistently related to each other" *(Terwogt & Hoeksma 1995)* and up to 90% of a customer's perception of a product or service is based on color alone *(Khattak et al. 2018)*. Therefore, by understanding and applying the psychology of color in your brand strategy you will be able to gain an aspect of control over your audience's brand perception, which will help you when guiding them through your brand experience. Let's take a moment to think about ideas associated with color. Red is used to represent *caution*, to identify when one needs to *stop*, or to direct one to an *emergency* exit. Now, think about the connection of red in primitive times and on an emotional level. Blood is red which alerts to harm, danger, or even power. Red is also a color that is associated with love. Why might that be? When observing photos of the human heart, what color do you generally see? Red. We all know that a graphical depiction of a heart represents love. These are very raw, emotion-evoking examples that give rise to a specific notion of the color red. It would lead one to believe that primitive associations with the color red may have lent an idea to our modern-day conception of this color.

Even in modern-day language, we use colors to describe emotions. "Green with envy." "She is so mad; she is seeing red." "He is feeling blue today." While an individual's perception of color is somewhat subjective, marketing recognizes that colors are quite universal when it comes to meaning and emotion.

Let's consider each basic color and a few examples of the emotions they evoke:

Red - Power, Love, Danger
Orange- Energy, Enthusiasm, Sociability
Yellow - Happiness, Warmth, Cheer
Green - Nature, Healing, Fresh
Blue - Trust, Order, Tranquility
Pink - Femininity, Sweet, Kindness
Purple - Regal, Mystery, Spiritual
Brown - Rugged, Simple, Organic
Black - Formal, Fear, Dramatic
White - Innocent, Clean, Simple, Honest

Understanding your brand's voice will help you better position your brand strategy when choosing a color for your business. You should select a hue that properly represents your brand's personality. For example, let's pretend that you are preparing to open a holistic plant shop. Your unique product offering is geared around the healing aspect of plants. While you appreciate the Zen, feminine, Mother Earth connection that your plants provide, you want the atmosphere of your establishment and voice of your brand to be upbeat and buzzing, with a cheerful brand tone. In this instance, you could consider several colors for branding. Green evokes feelings of freshness, health, and nature. Pink can be associated with the femininity and the kindness that Mother Nature suggests. Brown brings about thoughts of the organic ground and earth. Yellow helps to evoke a feeling of cheer and happiness. Because there are so many colors that could represent your holistic plant shop, you may find yourself a bit confused on which route to go. Hypothetically speaking, let's say you have decided that you want the voice and personality of your brand to take precedence, so you choose yellow for your primary brand color. I always recommend prioritizing tone and personality when choosing a primary brand color, but that does not mean that there isn't a place for secondary colors.

We know from our daily experiences with brand logos that brands often choose more than one color to represent their business. In the example above, you could choose a secondary color based on aspects of your unique product offering or you could resort to the color wheel to create an eye-catching brand color scheme. The color wheel is widely used to help creatives pair colors for the development of harmonious brand visuals. Depending on your strategy, you may choose a secondary color from the color wheel that is positioned opposite from your main brand color as a complementary color or a hue positioned within the same color family but of a different shade for a monochromatic scheme. Understanding the color wheel and color theory, as well as the implications of how color affects emotions, will not only help you create appealing brand visuals but will also help your customer to connect more deeply with your brand.

Unquestionably, color is a very important aspect of the brand visual. At the same time, researchers have determined that type font is also key for getting your brand's voice across to the market. "Type font characteristics indeed shape brand personality perceptions when consumers are unfamiliar with the brand." *(Grohmann et al, 2012).*

There are so many interactions that your customer will have with your business, such as with your website, brick-and-mortar store, social media, pop-up shop, business cards, brochures, and flyers to name a few. Thus, your brand logo and other visuals should accurately represent your business personality. Take time when choosing the font and color of your logo and brand materials.

When envisioning the tone and personality of my clothing store, I knew I wanted a clean, feminine vibe with a classy, formal aura. I chose to call it The Ivory Closet because the color ivory *(being close on the color wheel to white)* evokes a feeling of pristine and cleanliness. Because ivory is a hard color to print, as it does not show up on a white background, I used the formal aspect of my brand tone to further guide me to my primary logo color and typeface.

As with color, experts have identified that font categories too have personality traits:

Serif - Classic, Traditional, Trustworthy, Respectable
Sans-serif - Modern, Minimal, Clean, Universal
Slab serif - Bold, Dramatic, Confident, Strong
Script - Elegant, Sophisticated, Sincere, Friendly
Handwritten - Informal, Artistic, Personable
Decorative - Stylish, Distinctive, Unique, Fashionable

I chose a black, serif typeface for my logo, which exhibited class and formality. To evoke a mood of elegance, I chose a secondary logo typeface from the script font family. While not appearing in my logo, I often used light pink as a secondary color when creating other branded marketing materials to enhance the feminine tone of my brand.

With white-washed furniture, gold accents, light pink and ivory textiles, and light cream painted walls, I was able to create a branded atmosphere that perfectly matched the personality of my business.

Touch

According to studies by psychologists from Yale and Harvard Universities, texture is linked to abstract concepts, and touching an object with texture can influence a person's thoughts and how they make decisions *(Hsu, 2010)*. Touch is very essential during product development and when creating your business atmosphere from a brand perspective. For example, if you are creating a product people will hold in their hands or wear, you need to contemplate the texture of your product. When considering brand experience, the environment in which your client interacts with you will include several touch points that will influence your customer and develop their perception of your brand. For example, a salon owner can't overlook the comfort of their beauty chairs or underestimate the texture of the smocks their clients will be wearing. While this sense is often ignored when branding, touch is very important in the brand experience.

Smell

I must admit, I completely missed the mark when considering scent in the initial branding of my boutique. Initially, I thought of smell in terms of products such as candles or lotions, but never as a component of the brand strategy. One day, a friend dropped by my shop to pitch her new company. She was selling commercial scent machines and explaining how the machine could add an extension to the customer's brand experience via scent-activated memory. My young entrepreneur mindset didn't really believe that a scent could be so powerful but because she was my friend, I didn't want to say no, so I gave it a try. After testing more than 50 fragrances, I chose one that was clean, mildly femininely fruity with a classy vanilla undertone. It was an instant hit! From the very first day that I activated the scent machine in my shop the customers noticed. Eighty percent of the people who walked into my store immediately complimented the scent. Over the next six months, I would get comments from regulars about how they loved hanging The Ivory Closet clothing items in their closet as soon as they got home because the smell of the shop would permeate through their wardrobe.

Thinking back to how I chose the sound and name for my shop, I realize that the scent fit into my brand story all along. The brand idea began with my experiences in my closet, and now, through scent, my customers would experience The Ivory Closet in their closet long after leaving the store. The popularity of the scent grew and clients began requesting candles, soap, room sprays, and perfumes of The Ivory

Closet's signature scent. This led to the development of a fragrance line that quickly became one of the top-selling SKUs in the shop.

Looking back, scent may have been my customers' strongest link to my brand. The power of smell. Just think about it. Your client can experience your brand without even seeing your logo or being present in your selling space. Therefore I tout smell as one of the most important components of branding. Like color, smell is linked to emotion processing and memory. The unique and unexpected experience that smell delivers to the customers can leave them lingering in your space or around your brand for longer periods of time, which will help to enhance their perception of your business. If your strategy involves scent, the brand experience may continue for your client long after the purchase process is complete.

The 4 Senses Strategy In Action

Use the information that you have learned in my 4 Senses Strategy to brainstorm fonts, colors, sounds, smells, textures, and other creative aspects of your brand. Next, we will use your ideas to work on name development. Keep your brand personality and voice in mind when completing the following questions.

When imagining your brand or product, what adjectives or phrases best describe your brand voice and personality?

_____

_____

_____

_____

What would your brand sound like?

_____

_____

_____

_____

What colors best represent the voice and personality of your brand?

_____

_____

_____

_____

Which font category(s) best represent the voice and personality of your brand?

_____

_____

_____

_____

Research different fonts that exist in these categories and record your favorites below.

_____
_____
_____
_____
_____

List the physical touch points in which your client can interact with your brand. (Examples: pop-up shops, brick and mortars, or product features.)

_____
_____
_____
_____
_____

Are there ways in which you can enhance the brand experience by improving upon these touch points?

_____
_____

When imagining what your brand would smell like, list the adjectives below.

_____
_____

SECURING YOUR BRAND

Thus far we have discussed every aspect of the brand except the one that is most recognized by the consumer, the actual name of your brand. The reason why I took you through a journey of the senses before discussing your brand name, is because the 4 Senses Strategy adds a level of creativity to the branding process that is often overlooked when you begin developing your brand by first choosing a name. Also, in the current business landscape, you must worry about securing your brand way beyond just a business license. You will need to secure your business through a URL and on every popular social site. If you begin strategizing by choosing a name and checking its URL and social platform availability, you can get lost in the game of name availability, which removes creativity from the brand process completely.

Your brand name is almost always the first visual or audible element that the consumer will encounter with your company and therefore, it must make a great first impression. However, coming up with a brand name isn't as easy as choosing a cute phrase or unique word. There are so many aspects an entrepreneur must consider when choosing their brand identity, such as growth potential, brand-experience cohesion, and availability.

I know you have streamlined your thought process and are super excited about your new business venture, but when branding a business, it is smart to keep the name generalizable. A small business venture can easily grow into a mini-empire over time. Be sure to choose a brand name that can be flexible and not too specific. Originally only offering donuts, Dunkin' Donuts has expanded its business strategy outside of the breakfast market and has dropped "Donuts" from its logo. Dunkin' now caters to the lunch crowd and is officially competing in the fast-food market, offering frozen drinks, lunch, snacks, and more. Dunkin's current URL is dunkindonuts.com. Unfortunately, the URL dunkin.com is taken by another company. Perhaps in the future, Dunkin' will purchase the dunkin.com URL, but there are costs associated with domain purchasing, especially if the domain name is that of a multi-billion-dollar brand. While business is booming, it seems Dunkin' Donuts didn't consider the possibility of growing outside of the breakfast category when branding.

Imagine if Samsung branded itself as Samsung Grocery. Did you know that it began as a Korean grocery store in the 1930s? Now the company is widely known for electronics and home appliances.

As most of you know Amazon began as just an online bookseller. What a rebrand catastrophe it would face if it had chosen onlinebookseller.com as its name. If you have to rebrand a strong and solid name to better fit your growing business it may require you to retire a successful brand, absorb sunk costs, and spend a sizable amount of money rebuilding an entirely new brand. When naming your business, you should keep growth potential and future business opportunities in mind.

◆ ◆ ◆

Unconventional Wisdom
Experience is the evolution of brand and business.

◆ ◆ ◆

It is important to be sure that your customers feel a sense of cohesion between your brand experience and your brand name so that they will consider them one and the same. Brand-experience cohesion is when a customer hears or sees your brand name and they immediately remember their incredible experience with your business, and vice versa, if the customer has an incredible experience that is not related to your business, they compare that experience with the one they had with your brand.

One of my favorite brand experiences has been with The European Wax Center. I was pleasantly surprised when I entered the establishment for the first time. Because my prior experience with waxing was such a stark difference from The European Wax Center, I have never associated brow waxing with relaxation. I usually just pop in a reclining chair at the back of my nail salon for a quick wax followed by short-lived discomfort and red, itchy brows. The atmosphere at The European Wax Center immediately took me by surprise. The lobby was clean and comforting, a fresh scent permeated the air, and there were lots of great beauty products to peruse. I was greeted with very knowledgeable and friendly staff who explained all of my waxing options and even taught me a few new things about the waxing process. The waxing rooms were private and inviting. The aesthetician thoroughly explained the process as she performed the service, which really put me at ease. After strategically shaping my brows to complement my facial frame, she used specialized products that greatly minimized the discomfort and swelling that goes along with waxing. When I hear the brand name, The European Wax Center, I immediately think of my experience, which was pleasant, informative, and relaxing. While the brand name, The European Wax Center, is fairly long and would not allow for them to easily expand into service categories outside of waxing, my experience was so memorable that I instantly think of The European Wax Center when talking about brows and even when I have a similar pleasant encounter with another, non-competing company. My mind has assigned a pleasant, informative, and relaxing service experience with The European Wax Center brand name and therefore, I have developed brand-experience cohesion. When naming your business, keep in mind the experience that you want your customers to remember. Choose a name that is memorable and can easily evoke positive emotions from your client's encounter with your business.

Now that you have completed the 4 Senses Strategy, and you have a solid vision in your head about your brand's visuals and personality, how do you bring that vision to fruition by choosing a business name? Earlier we used The 4 Senses Strategy to aid in developing your brand within each individual sense, however, it is also a great tool to utilize when assigning a name to your business as it will help to place you in your brand space before it even exists. One very unconventional strategy for materializing your vision is through the use of interior design. After completing the 4 Senses Strategy for a client, I like to go through interior design magazines and cut out room designs that align with my brand color, tone, and personality. Then, I create a vision board by gluing those cutouts on a poster board. I also include aspects from the 4 Senses Strategy on my vision board, such as color, smell, font, music, and texture. This visualization activity is very useful during the naming process. The idea here is to create a tangible aspect of your brand from the visualizations of your mind's eye. When brainstorming names, you can use the vision board to guide you.

Once you have come up with a few brand name ideas, it is very important to research the availability of those names' URLs and social platform identifiers. Depending on your brand and business strategy, you may want to search for trademark availability as well. For my makeup line, I created a product portfolio without researching trademark availability and ended up having to rebrand a year and a half into the life of my product because another company had trademarked my brand name in the same product category. Sure, I could have fought it in court with proof that my brand existed first; however, the court and attorney fees that would have come along with the lawsuit trumped what was in the bank for my newly growing brand. Lesson learned. In the rebranding process for my product line, I was sure to check all the availability boxes before re-launching the brand.

Ready to secure your brand with an official name? Next, you will complete the *Name That Brand* exercise which will help you give your business identity with a brand name.

Name That Brand

To begin the brainstorming process of securing your brand name, we will be going through a few steps to help you develop a memorable and connected brand name.

Think back to humanizing your brand. Observe the 4 Senses Strategy questionnaire that you completed in the previous section. Write down at least 10 brand names that derive from this brainstorming activity.

_____

_____

_____

_____

_____

After completing the task above, go online and research "interior design styles." Look through all the living space images. Create a vision board with design styles that match your brand voice and personality.

Write down at least five additional brand names that come to mind while viewing your vision board.

_____

_____

_____

_____

_____

91

Review the brand names that you have come up with. Can some of these be meshed together? Do you like some aspects more than others?

Be sure that the brand name you choose is:

Easy to spell.
When people want to check out your business online, they are going to have to know how to spell your business when typing in the URL or researching via a search engine. I always advise my clients against quirky, misspelled words. While it can look cute and fun, misspelled words are hard to remember and may cause confusion when new customers seek out your brand.

Not to long.
Your URL is generally after the @ in your email. If you choose a super-long brand name, your customers will have to type out that entire URL, every time they email you, which can be frustrating. (I would consider my email address too long but I have built significant brand equity so it would be a mistake to reset it. Learn from my error.)

Easy to pronounce.
Once your brand has taken off, it would be an epic fail if half of your clients were excitedly spreading the news but not pronouncing your brand name correctly. Names that are hard to pronounce may be hard to spell.

Now it's time to check availability.

Go to GoDaddy.com and enter your brand name into the URL search. This will tell you if your brand name is available for your website URL.

Research social sites to check your brand name availability. Try to secure the same social name across all platforms. This really helps to create an omnichannel branded experience *(which we will discuss more about in Part 4.)*

You don't want an outsider posing as your brand on social media so you should secure your brand name on all of the major social platforms regardless of if you plan to be active on those platforms. Taking ownership of your brand name at each digital touch point will give you greater brand security.

Go to Trademark.gov and check the availability of your brand name.

PITCH PERFECT

Imagine that you pop into an elevator. The door opens on the second floor and Lori Greiner from Shark Tank steps in. It is just you and Lori. Now you have the perfect, however extremely unexpected, opportunity to engage Lori in conversation about a new product that you are launching before the elevator reaches the tenth floor. The only problem is, you are completely unprepared and are at a loss for words, so instead, you ride the elevator quietly until you reach your destination. Huge, missed opportunity!

Every unconventional entrepreneur must have a compelling and carefully constructed pitch ready to go at all times. I know this seems a bit inauthentic or "salesy" and many traditional pitches do fit that bill; however, an unconventional entrepreneur doesn't "sell" to their audience. Instead, the unconventional entrepreneur constructs a pitch that is both engaging and uniquely conversational.

◆◆◆

Unconventional Wisdom
Just like an award-winning choir must perfect their
pitch, so must the successful entrepreneur.

◆◆◆

Traditionally, a pitch, or "elevator pitch," is a brief 30-second introduction consisting of an explanation of what you and your business do, your unique selling point, and a call to action. Very regimented, right? I remember in my undergrad days having to get up in front of the class and ramble off a 30-second elevator pitch, tongue-tied and twisted, trying to hit all the touch points in such a short amount of time. Eventually, after landing a corporate sales job, my pitch became effortless, eloquently flowing from my mouth without even having to think about what I was saying. I had finally edited a graceful pitch that would generalize to my target market and could be delivered at a moment's notice, yet there was one problem. My pitch was heavily sales-focused. In traditional business settings, this type of pitch can work and may even be expected, but as an unconventional entrepreneur, your marketing tactic is not to sell to the customer but to be relatable and connect with your client instead. An engaging pitch that creatively reveals the unexpected aspect of a business offering is much to be admired. Your pitch should spark interest in your audience and leave them wanting to know more. A perfectly executed pitch will open the door for additional communication and possible opportunities.

Let's revisit our organic plant shop example. If I were the owner of this company, my pitch might sound something like this:

EXAMPLE PITCH

Have you ever been so stressed that you can't sleep, or worse your heart races? Well, my passion is developing organic, medicinal plants which help to reduce the number of doctor's visits needed by healing hundreds of common and not-so-common ailments. I have experienced so much relief from these plants that I have made it my life's work.

This pitch is unique in that it attempts to engage and connect with the audience by asking a question. Stress is common among many people and therefore the odds that the audience can't relate to the question asked in this pitch is very low. In fact, the person would likely respond that they can totally relate and may even offer up a situation in which they experienced restless sleep due to stress. By first asking a question you open the door for engaging communication, trust building, and bonding between yourself and your audience.

The second part of this pitch reveals how you are solving these problems through your passion and dedicated work. Notice how the words "passion" and "life's work" evoke a feeling of emotion, deep knowledge, and expertise when you listen to this pitch? Much like being the face of your brand and establishing expertise to solve your clients' problems, your elevator pitch works in conjunction to do the same. After hearing this pitch, the listener will likely engage further and, in that moment, you can further introduce yourself and your business, as well as tell them more about that lavender plant that was bred to help reduce high stress levels and induce better sleep.

What are you doing to change the world? What are you doing to change your client's lifestyle? Your pitch should solve problems and introduce life-changing solutions for your target demographic. The elevator pitch should be captivating, interesting, and informative to the receiver.

Next, we will study the components needed to craft an unconventional, captivating pitch, which will not only instantly grab your audience's attention, but also will have them asking questions so that they can better connect with you and your brand. Think along the lines of putting the idea, or solution, in the consumer's mind.

Introduction

Traditional elevator pitches instruct you to first introduce yourself and your business. I believe that this approach is predictable and sounds too much like an advertisement. Your listener will immediately know they are being propositioned and will likely tune out. Leave the introductions for the end of your pitch. If the listener shows interest, they will probably initiate the introduction and inquire more about your business. Remember, everyone likes their own ideas.

Ask A Question

Have you ever heard the theory that everyone likes their own ideas? By asking a question, you engage the listener, which gets their wheels turning. They will start to consider how your question fits into their life and their particular needs. This will spark a heightened interest in the customer.

Solve a Problem

Briefly touch on how your brand can solve their problem so that they may internally conceptualize how your product may fit their needs. If the listener offers up additional insight after you asked your question, cater the rest of your interaction to solve their specific problem. Make your brand the hero. Offer up your expertise on how your business can be the simple fix to the issue at hand.

To use our last example, let's assume the listener does have problems sleeping. Suppose they use lavender oils on their head to help relax the mind before bedtime. When hearing the elevator pitch above, the idea of a lavender plant has been introduced. Since the listener drinks hot tea before bed, perhaps they would ask more about how the plant can be used to help make their tea more personalized to solve their restless sleep problem, which leaves the door wide open for a more extensive introduction and meaningful conversation.

Constructing Your Elevator Pitch

What question will you ask? Be sure to construct a question that is generalizable to your target market.

How will your business solve your client's problem?

_____

_____

How will you naturally introduce yourself at the end of your pitch?

_____

_____

Notes:

_____

_____

_____

_____

_____

_____

_____

_____

_____

_____

IV
GETTING THE
JOB DONE

It is execution time! Up to this point, you have built upon your elements and created a standout brand. Now it is time to get the job done. In Part 4, you will learn tips for streamlining productivity, which will help provide balance between your personal and work life. You will also develop a strategy for monetizing your business, launching your brand across multiple mediums to achieve the omnichannel experience, and ways to build your network for camaraderie and growth.

NEVER TIP THE SCALES

Before we jump into the meat of Part 4 — monetizing your business, mediums for brand exposure, and building your network — it is essential for any entrepreneur to understand the importance of setting boundaries and creating processes for optimal productivity in both your work and personal life. So many businessmen and women learn the hard way. Failing to set and respect processes and boundaries can lead to resentment, burnout, extreme disorganization, and in worst-case scenarios, health issues and/or business failure.

This story is going to be very uncomfortable for me as I have never publicly revealed my part in the downfall of my first marriage, yet it is an important story to share. I hear so many versions of this tale in the entrepreneurial community. My story is the perfect example of how imbalance can shatter your personal life and business dreams in an instant. While my first husband and I equally had a hand in the destruction of our marriage, my goal here is not to finger point, only to candidly share the truth of how I allowed my business passion to become a factor in the dismantling of my family. I am going to be completely transparent and overshare to the point of embarrassment, but hopefully this will hit home for a fellow unconventional entrepreneur and act as a disruptor for change.

It was 2015, our son was 6 months old, and the wedding was upon us. Yes, we started a family before marriage, but by now, it should be no surprise that even in marriage, I was a bit unconventional. By this time, I had owned and operated The Ivory Closet for three years. It was my five-year plan to grow my brand into a mini business empire by franchising The Ivory Closet and expanding my business portfolio with another store brand concept. I had my sights set on an end goal and mad determination to bring this dream to fruition. There was one problem, a problem that ultimately cost me everything. My limitless goals went from "idea" to "finish line" without considering each vital step necessary to keep the balance between my family and work life.

After we said, "I do," I continued to work day in and day out, full steam ahead, completely enveloped in my passion, with an unwavering focus on achieving my entrepreneurial dream. I prioritized being a mother and business owner first, failing to reorganize my efforts to include the needs of my new husband. I was determined to achieve my expected outcome while all along neglecting the process.

◆ ◆ ◆

Unconventional Wisdom
Do not neglect, yet respect and perfect.

◆ ◆ ◆

The business grew rapidly, with a total of five The Ivory Closet locations and one new boutique brand, The Attic Apparel. Three of the five The Ivory Closet boutiques were franchised, and I owned the other three shops. Because of the sudden rapid growth in location and staff, I set up corporate headquarters in a small office warehouse space downtown for centralized operations. My dreams were starting to materialize right before my eyes. We had great employees, wonderful interns, lovely franchise owners, super loyal customers, and I was thrilled to have an official office space and corporate warehouse. My intern, assistant, and I worked countless hours in our downtown offices supporting our franchises, ordering company-wide inventory, developing corporate marketing campaigns, managing our influencers, conducting bi-weekly photo shoots, running our e-commerce business, and shipping online orders, among other things. It became apparent very quickly that I needed more help and since the shops were more lucrative than my spouse's business at the time, he stepped in part time to take over managing operations at The Attic Apparel. I was very appreciative and felt a great sense of relief, but before I knew it, we were at each other's throats. We began to lose our individuality and our identities, the very things that drew us together in the first place.

Although I knew things weren't all peachy keen at home, when we decided to expand our family with baby number two, I had no choice but to keep up the pace. My oldest was in full-time preschool while my youngest became my workday companion. I set up a playpen and diaper changing station in my office downtown and continued daily operations with an infant, just as I had done with my oldest before preschool. It was definitely a challenge feeding a baby while on conference calls, changing diapers in between steaming clothing from a new shipment, and running photoshoots with my little guy strapped to my chest. Looking back, I must have been insane, but my unwavering focus to achieve this dream kept me fueled. From an outsider's viewpoint, this persistence may elicit inspiration, but ultimately, for me, it resulted in defeat. My role as a mother and business owner was very important to me, and what little energy I had left, after a long day at work, was poured into my children. I knew that I wanted to achieve the perfect family, financial stability, and a thriving business empire but I never took the appropriate steps to perfect the process, set boundaries, and maintain a balance between my work and personal life. Ultimately, my spouse and I decided to go our separate ways.

While my ex-husband has always been 100% present in our children's lives and is an excellent father, our family under one household had ceased to exist. In an instant, I was a single mom. I tried to keep up the pace, but it quickly became clear, I just couldn't do it all. The financial struggle to maintain my previous lifestyle created crippling mental pressure. I knew I had business assets that I could sell to keep my personal assets in check, and vice versa, yet selling my business assets meant selling part of my dream, and selling my personal assets meant selling stability. I officially came face to face with financial ruin. I knew I needed to act fast to relieve the pressure before the balloon popped and the confetti fell to my feet. Not the kind of party I had planned for my life. Of course, I felt really sorry for myself, but there was no time for reactive tears. I needed to become proactive and come up with a plan to not only preserve but entwine my personal and business life. It was time to perfect the process, set boundaries, and make some really hard, and somewhat humbling, decisions.

In order to establish balance, I was forced to relinquish a large portion of what I had sacrificed so much to create. To reduce overhead, I closed my corporate offices and downsized into one store location. I sold my house and purchased a new home, which allowed me to put back a little cash. To help with health insurance, child care, and monthly food expenses for our six-month and three-year-old boys, I signed up for the Woman, Infants, and Children *(WIC)*, and other government assistance programs which provided health insurance and childcare. Through this experience, I learned a very important and valuable lesson that has not only made me grow stronger as a person but has humbled me as a successful unconventional entrepreneur, "Nothing is beneath me."

◆ ◆ ◆

Unconventional Wisdom
Nothing is beneath you.

◆ ◆ ◆

Now that I was better positioned financially, it was time to perfect the process and set boundaries. Of course, I could always give up and go back to work for a corporation, but I just wasn't ready to throw in the towel. While this entire experience chipped away at my confidence, leaving me to heavily doubt myself and my abilities as a businesswoman and adult in general, my determination, or hard-headedness as some might say, forced my nose back to the grindstone. I completed my master's degree in business, consulted with several shops on operations and marketing outside of my own stores, made a small, albeit steady, income on my blog, and had built around ten e-commerce and commercial business websites. After pumping myself up enough to relight a fire under my ass and regaining confidence that my know-how and skill set were solid, I began to rewrite my future.

While your work and personal life journey may not be anything like mine, this story is a prime example of how any entrepreneur can hit rock bottom by not ensuring balance between the two.

◆◆◆

Unconventional Wisdom
Never tip the scales.

◆◆◆

Perfecting The Process
To rewrite my future, I began to brainstorm more efficient and effective ways to use my expertise. I knew that I needed to reorganize my business offering as well as the flow between my work and personal life. But a flow without a process doesn't achieve a particular end.

A *flow* in itself is like a process. You start from point A and go to point B, but then to points C, D, E, and F without acknowledging the effects in between. A *process* mirrors a flow yet it differs in that, in a process, the flow has a cognitive aspect to its direction with a particular end in mind. From my story, I am sure you can gather that this was fatal flaw number one. I had been operating in flow mode absent of any structured process.

flow - go from one place to another in a steady stream. (Oxford Lexico)

process - a series of actions or steps taken in order to achieve a particular end. (Oxford Lexico)

While business processes are essential to success, in this section, we are going to talk specifically about the importance of acknowledging the flow and perfecting the process between work and personal life to achieve a mutually beneficial end goal. In perfecting the process, you will consider both your personal and family life as one in the same for defining goals. Simply stating your desired outcome and going full speed to the finish line without a plan will result in a chaotic flow, internal stress, the inability to make rational decisions, and ultimately, a lack of control. To establish and maintain a clear direction for your company and your personal life, you must first set mutually beneficial goals and then acknowledge the proper steps necessary to achieve those outcomes.

As I desperately brainstormed ways to pull myself from what felt like a bottomless pit and reflected on where I had gone wrong, I came to a realization. When did I ever stop to consider the steps I would need to take to achieve my goals? Why did I have so many goals that sent me in so many different directions? Business goals, family goals, spiritual goals, social goals, and individual goals, all were achievable but none could be achieved because they weren't in alignment. My life had several paths working towards different outcomes, which had me burning the candle at both ends in an effort to achieve some sort of satisfaction. The minute I realized that I needed to stop the mindless flow and merge these paths to target the same end results was the moment I entered a state of strategic resurgence. It was an incredibly enlightening moment, as if a secret "how-to" map had suddenly appeared in front of me to vanquish all hopelessness and fear. It wasn't that I couldn't do it, I was just doing it all wrong. I was so relieved to know that all was not lost, and I had not been defeated.

After the epiphany, I reflected on aspects of my personal life as a whole. I am a firm believer that a healthy work-life balance begins with the personal side of things. If you are truly happy with your family, individual, spiritual, and social life, your appreciation for these things will remind you to always keep them as a priority and you will be less likely to let your passion invade.

passion - a strong and barely controllable emotion. (Oxford Reference)

I know, it seems that I am placing a negative connotation on passion, which really isn't the case. I am just pointing out that *passion* is a very powerful, almost uncontrollable emotion. While life is only half lived without passion, don't let your passion rule you. Much of the unconventional entrepreneurial world is learning to get out of your own way but there are also times, especially when passion is present, when you must realize when to pull back on the reins.

◆ ◆ ◆

Unconventional Wisdom
Learn to get out of your own way while also knowing when to pull back on the reins.

◆ ◆ ◆

Personal Reflection
To start the process of strategic goal alignment between your personal and work life, you must first take some time to reflect on your current personal life situation and how you may want it to change or remain the same. In areas of your personal life in which you strive for change, pinpoint what is lacking and brainstorm ways to fill the void. What do you like and dislike about your current personal situation? What is lacking and what resolution would fill the void?

When I started the personal reflection process, I created a Personal Reflection Chart to keep my thoughts organized and to refer back to when goal setting. This activity taught me so many things about what I truly wanted out of my personal life and how to align my business goals to match those aspirations.

I have included my Personal Reflection Chart from 2017, when I almost lost it all. We will use this as an example for understanding the personal reflection activity so that you will have a clear direction when completing your own Personal Reflection Chart.

Personal Reflection Chart Example

	Like	Dislike	Lacking	Resolution
Family	Making Memories Love	Growing Fast and Missing Out	Quality Time	More Activities & Trips
Individual	Determined Independent	Anxiety & Fear Unhealthy No Time to Think	Selfcare Time	Schedule Time for Meditation, Spa, & to be Alone In Thought
Spiritual	Enlightened Mind Faith Less Worry	NOTHING!	Practice	Find a Church or Spiritual Support Group
Social	Belong to a Pack Support	Could Be Creating Distance	No Time to See My Friends	Plan a Weekly Dinner or Coffee Date With Friends

Family

The biggest joy in my life is spending time with my husband and children. While living and working as a single mother, my children were always around, yet the time I spent with them felt passive and thoughtless. Of course, I have always taken time to love on them and tell them that they are my world, but during that period I never felt fully present. I needed to keep working hard so that I could continue to give them the life I felt they deserved, but this came with huge sacrifices. They grow up so fast and the window of opportunity to savor these fleeting moments was quickly closing. As a single mother, I knew what I had to do to provide financially, but the realization of their childhood dissipating right before my eyes was earth-shattering. I wanted to be present, plan more exciting activities, take more trips, or simply enjoy a movie night at home with them. I was majorly lacking quality time.

Individual

Being an independent and determined person has pushed me to take risks without much consideration for failure because I know deep down, I will never let myself hit the ground. However, during this trying period, feelings of self-doubt and fear were becoming ever present in my day-to-day life had become ever-present. For the first time ever, I experienced anxiety attacks. With work and parenting, I was always under pressure to act quickly with no time to think, recharge, or even care for myself. While I wouldn't call myself a health nut as far as diet goes, before my divorce I had always taken time to recharge by hitting the gym and practicing self-care. My health slowly declined, and I knew the debilitating anxiety attacks would continue if I didn't create an escape for the stress.

Spiritual

It is going to sound crazy, but I have always felt like I was on another spectrum when it comes to my spirituality. Since childhood, I have had this feeling inside that God was always there and through him, I can conquer anything. As we grow older, sadly, our pure little souls become stained with negative experiences, and that light, while always there, grows dim in our eyes. I had put my spirituality last in line. Before I knew it, it was as if my spiritual path was covered in brush, no longer clear to lead the way to God. I was losing sight of my beliefs. To reestablish my practice, I needed to find a church and leadership group close to my new home.

Social

My friends are absolutely incredible. Before children, I was always on the social scene, staying involved in many different organizations. As a result, I made a wonderfully eclectic group of lifelong friends, but naturally, when one has children and settles down, the social life gets put on the back burner. Of course, our priorities shift when we build a family, but as you will learn in a later chapter, everyone needs a village. Even as far back as 8,000 years ago, humans realized the benefits of village settlements for security, sharing tasks, and camaraderie. Having trustworthy friends outside of family can help with coping, loneliness, mental stability, and feeling like you belong. Because I didn't have time for my friends, I was constantly worried that our relationships were strained, and also felt isolated during this very desperate time. It is important to be around those who truly know you, "can speak your language," help you triumph through the good, and work through the bad in life. While my children came first, I also needed to carve out time for relationships outside of my family. But how?

After completing my Personal Reflection Chart, it was obvious that there were so many family, individual, spiritual, and social aspects of my life that intersected with each other. Planning for time with friends would reduce loneliness and create a sense of support, which could help reduce individual anxiety and fear. Spiritual practice also helps to reduce my anxiety while providing a sense of enlightenment. My children truly light up my life, and any quality time spent with them fills me with happiness, appreciation, and love. When I am not fearful and anxious, my confidence, determination, and independence are fueled.

This assessment really helped to steer me in the right direction for cohesiveness in my personal life, yet there was one underlying problem that could not be resolved through brainstorming aspects of my personal life. When I reviewed my resolutions, I realized that I couldn't execute them due to a lack of time. Lack of time prevented me from making memories with my children, taking care of myself, or planning activities with friends. I questioned "How do I reclaim time to balance my personal life? Where was my time being stolen?" Deep down, I knew exactly where the imbalance of time was distributed. It was in my business. *(Scan the code below to get your Personal Reflections Worksheet.)*

Once you uncover the obstacle(s) that prevent you from streamlining your personal life, you will begin the mutual goal planning process to better align your personal and work life. If the obstacle uncovered in your Personal Reflections Worksheet cannot be fixed through your work life, you may have to search outside of work to uncover other aspects of your life that can be improved upon. Either way, this activity will help you to a gain deeper insight into your true personal wants and needs, so that you can ensure balance when goal setting.

Many of you could be just starting out with your company while others are established entrepreneurs reading along for a meaningful transition into the unconventional entrepreneur lifestyle. Either way, streamlined goal setting will help you to increase productivity in all aspects of your life.

Streamlined Goal Setting

As you can see, I had identified several resolutions on my Personal Reflections Worksheet but given the situation in both my work and personal life, I had no way of actually executing those resolutions. Through the Personal Reflection Activity, I was able to expose *time* as the overarching issue preventing me from streamlining my goals. I was directing a huge imbalance of time to my work over my personal life. If time was not being spent with family, friends, spiritually, or on myself, it was being allotted to my business activities. This is when I began step two in the process of balancing.

I knew what I wanted out of my personal life and understood that I needed to reclaim time, but what about my business passion? I had spent more than ten, self-taught years expanding my skill set to cultivate growth in several different markets, but did I really enjoy my business dealings in each market, or was I just confident and comfortable with the work? While my clothing store originally sprung from passion, in recent years I had fallen out of love with the day-to-day tasks. I felt like I was just going through the motions without any excitement. I loved writing and creating content for my blog; however, I was so focused on growing my shop through my blog platform that all of my content was geared around fashion without much variation in the topics that I truly enjoyed writing about. I attended and blogged about local fashion events, set up pop-up shops, and met up with other fashion bloggers for consignment sales in an effort to grow my boutique brand. It was always fun, but I couldn't ignore the void that was growing in my personal life. While my early years of owning my own clothing store, before children and a failed marriage, made me feel whole, my life and passion as a single mother had transitioned my state of mind. Ignoring this change only increased the imbalance between work and personal life. My personal life had evolved to include a family, which changed my source of happiness.

Happiness was no longer solely derived from my business successes and accomplishments, instead it was primarily gained through time spent with my children and my role as a mother. Despite knowing this, I foolishly pressed forward, striving to accomplish the goals I had set for my business. Little by little my efforts to accomplish these goals began to feel like I was trudging through mud, which got thicker by the day. I didn't want to give up on my business empire dreams because deep down it felt like I would be giving up on myself. It felt like failure, something I had vowed to remove from my mindset. I had not yet realized that what I wanted as a 26-year-old woman versus what I wanted at the age of 33 had completely turned on its head. Nevertheless, my stubborn brain was fixated on the outdated objective. Luckily, my unhappiness grew to an unbearable point, which forced me to take a step back and seriously reevaluate every aspect of my life. Much to my surprise, after I reflected on my personal life through the Personal Reflection Activity and identified that lack of time was creating anxiety and preventing me from achieving many of my personal goals, I came to the conclusion that my work life had to change. While the seven years of owning and growing my brand in retail were pure heaven for quite some time I had grown out of my old passion and into a new phase in my unconventional journey.

In order to reclaim time, I needed to reevaluate and reorganize my business strategy. As I mentioned before, I loved writing and creating content for my blog and social platforms and luckily for me, the content I had created started to bring in money. This proved there was financial potential in being an influencer, but I knew that I wouldn't achieve monetization on a larger scale if my content wasn't thoughtfully created with transparency and passion. I needed to restructure my content calendar to include topics that fueled my creativity and excitement. I decided to rebrand and expand my blog to appeal to a larger audience through the coverage of more lifestyle topics, rather than primarily fashion posts.

In my time as a boutique owner, I enjoyed mentoring other retail business owners. I had learned so many tips and tricks for small business retail sales, marketing, and customer service over the years, and delighted in helping other local businesses strategize. In fact, during this time, two shop owners reached out asking if I would consult them and if so, to send over my rates. How exciting. What if I started consulting with local businesses while also focusing on rapidly growing the blog? The thought of it made me feel like a giddy high school girl going on her first date. I knew this feeling, and not because I had experienced it on my first date. It was the same feeling I had when making the decision seven years prior to leave corporate America and start my own shop. The realization that my time with The Ivory Closet was coming to an end was a bittersweet moment in my life and one I will never forget. Honestly, at this very moment, as I write, I have tears in my eyes. I had come a long way from being a single girl with a wild idea, fearful of failure but not too afraid to make the jump. I thought about the times in the very beginning of owning my shop in which I happily worked seven days a week, nine hours a day to make my dream become bigger than I had ever imagined. While my marriage had ended, I thought about the night I got engaged in my shop and all my friends who were there to surprise me. The memories of raising my little boys running around the store while I spoke with patrons flooded my mind. My oldest loved using the scanner to check out clients while at work with mommy. When my brother died, customers sent flowers to the store and even grieved in the shop with me. I wasn't saying goodbye to a job. I was closing the door to my entire adulthood as I had known it and the only creative passion, I had ever experienced in my life up to that point, yet I did it willfully and happily. Selling The Ivory Closet wasn't a failure, it was growth. My passion and what I wanted out of life had changed and I needed to set new goals that would satisfy all aspects of my life to ensure that the imbalance of time would never be an issue again. With my new business path planned, I began the goal-setting process.

goal setting – "a process that starts with careful consideration of what you want to achieve and ends with a lot of hard work to actually do it. In between, there are some very well-defined steps that transcend the specifics of each goal. Knowing these steps will allow you to formulate goals that you can accomplish." (Mindtools.com)

Setting top-line goals that are mutually beneficial for your personal and work life will ensure balance while you pursue your passion. When setting goals, you must identify what you want out of both your personal and work life and then pinpoint the smaller actions that need to be taken to achieve your desired outcome. Carefully planning the steps in between setting and achieving your goals can help you uncover streamlining processes along the way.

On the next page, you will find the Goal Attainment Worksheet that I completed after finishing my first Personal Reflection activity. Notice that I am not setting five- or ten-year goals here. While the practice of long-term goal setting is absolutely beneficial for the business side of things, when strategically planning to satisfy both your personal and work life, short-term, actionable goals are always best. First, I will explain the example provided, and then I will share a code for you to download your own Goal Attainment Worksheet. This activity will give you a foundation for your weekly schedule to help ensure balance.

My Goal Attainment Worksheet Example

Goal	Satisfies	How To Achieve	Weekly Work Time	Reward	Re-Evaluate
2 Family Trips Per Year	Personal	Schedule 2 weeks per year to travel	NA	Happiness & Quality Time	Annually
Expand Blog Into Travel Topics	Biz	Reach out to city travel bureaus for collabs. 3 Travel posts /yr	1 hr.	Biz Growth $$$	Annually
2 Consulting Clients Per Qtr	Biz	Pitch consulting biz 1 potential client meeting / wk	4 hr.	$$$	3 months
1 hr. of Selfcare Per Week	Personal	Every Tues. at 8pm turn phone on silent and take selfcare time	NA	Less Anxiety Promotes Health	1 month
Expand Blog Into Health & Beauty	Biz	2 Health & Beauty blog posts per month Pitch to health & beauty brands	2 hr.	Biz Growth $$$	1 month
Attend Church 3x's Per Month Minimum	Personal	Find church No work on Sunday	NA	Enlightenment Faith	2 months
Be Present in the Evening with my children	Personal	Hard stop with work at 6pm latest Sat. 8-12pm for overflow	NA	Happiness Qualtiy Time	1 month
Social Time 2x's Per Month with Friends	Personal	Reserve every other Wed.night to hang with friends.	NA	Support Happiness	1 month
Grow Brand in Local Community	Biz	Attend 2 social events per month	1 hr.	Brand Growth $$$	3 months
Rapidly Expand Blog & Influencer Brand	Biz	2-3 blog posts per week 1 IG/FB post per day 2 photoshoots per week 5-10 branded collabs per month	25 hrs.	$$$	1 month

Total Weekly Work Hours: 33 HOURS

Of course, many would say the ideal work week would not exceed 40 hours. For many entrepreneurs without employees or with a small staff, this may not be feasible at first. The main objective in goal planning is to set realistic, attainable goals. When assigning time between my business and personal life, I wanted to be sure that I allotted enough time in each area to comfortably achieve my objectives. While my "weekly work time," according to my Goal Attainment worksheet, added up to 33 hours, my business goals did not account for administrative tasks and other unforeseen daily work duties. In order to remain realistic after completing my Goal Attainment Worksheet, I set my maximum workweek time to 45 hours and even built in an emergency net, designating Saturday mornings from 8 a.m. to 12 p.m. for tasks that did not get done throughout the week but could not wait until the following week to be completed. With 45 hours a week designated to work, this left roughly 48 waking hours allocated to my personal life. While this may seem like a lot of time dedicated to work, as time goes on you will learn to streamline your business activities, which will reduce your working hours.

Notice how several of my personal and business goals overlap. For example, "two family trips per year" and "expand blog into travel topics," or "one hour of self-care per week" and "expand blog into health and beauty," or "social time two times per month with friends" and "grow brand locally." If I expand to cover travel topics on my blog, I will be scheduling trips in which I can take my family. Likewise, if I expand my blog to cover health and beauty topics, I can try new products for review while pampering. To achieve growing my brand locally, I will attend fun social events to which I can bring my friends. This is the perfect example of how perfecting the process can help you to streamline your business and personal life to instill a balance between the two.

Now I want to direct your attention to the reward column. After completing your goal attainment worksheet, be sure to evaluate the reward column to ensure that everything you want and need out of life, mentally and physically, is present. For example, happiness appears a couple of times in my reward column. Happiness is clearly a personal need for me but imagine if it did not appear in any of the reward blocks after completing my Goal Attainment worksheet. In order to make certain that you are perfecting the process, evaluate your rewards to ensure your mental and physical needs are being met. If you notice a need that is absent, brainstorm goals that would reward you with that need and include them in your Goal Attainment Worksheet. From my story, you can probably tell that happiness was rare at that time of my life, but it was a personal need that I craved to regain. If after I completed my Goal Attainment Worksheet happiness wasn't present in any of the reward blocks, perhaps I could refer back to my Personal Assessment Chart to brainstorm a goal that would reward me with happiness.

It is also important to set reminders for reevaluation of your goals. What you plan to do and the expected outcomes may differ when put into practice. No need to fret. Simply adjust your goal to be more realistic so that it fits comfortably within your lifestyle. I recommend revisiting your Personal Reflection and Goal Attainment worksheets often, as they will continue to evolve as your business grows and when there are new introductions to your personal life.

Since remarrying and expanding my business portfolio to focus more on mentorship, my Personal Reflections worksheet has changed to include marital goals while my Goal Attainment Worksheet now includes mentorship strategies. Since I have spent three years building my blog, I do not need to pitch to brands as much anymore. This has allowed me to significantly reduce my time in the *"rapidly expand blog and influencer brand"* area of my Goal Attainment Worksheet so that I can focus on helping other aspiring entrepreneurs.

As you can see, the process of personal reflection and goal planning will add a layer of transparency to your personal and work life to give you a level of control for ensuring a balance between the two. *(Scan the code below to get your Goal Attainment Worksheet.)*

Setting Boundaries

Now that you know all about fatal flaw number one, want to know what fatal flaw number two was? Fatal flaw number two was the failure to set boundaries. We have already laid the groundwork for setting boundaries with the processes above, now you must acknowledge which boundaries need to be put into play and strictly abide by them to maintain a healthy equilibrium between your work and personal life. When I remarried, I made a point to not only set boundaries between my personal life and work activities, but I communicated those boundaries with Greg, my husband, which instilled a level of mental accountability my on part.

There are many boundaries you can establish for a healthier lifestyle. For example, time assignment is generally a huge struggle for entrepreneurs, therefore the practice of setting strict, yet attainable weekly work hours will ensure that you do not neglect your personal life. This has been a saving grace for my second marriage. Since I am working with creativity and passion every day, I truly love my job, which makes it super hard to put down the pen when my husband comes home. My husband is such an incredible man and I definitely do not want to make the same mistake of neglecting my spouse's needs once again, therefore I not only shut down work by 6 p.m. or sooner, but I plan movie nights and date nights weekly to guarantee our honeymoon phase never dies.

Another boundary that can be made is reserving work calls for work time only. Even though my workday ends at 6 p.m., I often get work-related calls and emails well into the evening. Shutting down all work-related communication while enjoying personal time will not only help you to recharge so that you may be productive the next day but will prevent burnout as well.

◆ ◆ ◆

Unconventional Wisdom
Stay in your lane.

◆ ◆ ◆

My favorite boundary is "staying in your lane." Give yourself permission to decline opportunities that do not suit you or fit into your business passion. This may be hard, as many opportunities come with a potential monetary reward; however, as the old saying goes, you can't be everything to everyone. In other words, you can't accept every single opportunity that comes your way or you will not have the capacity to put your all into what makes your life truly great which is your work-life passion and personal time. You want to be great at what you do, right? So, don't pile your plate a mile high with tasks that don't make sense for your business or personal life. How about, don't pile your plate a mile high at all!

◆ ◆ ◆

Unconventional Wisdom
Be kind to yourself.

◆ ◆ ◆

Be kind to yourself. This may sound so simple, but it is something that I have to remind myself of constantly. "If I can just get this one more thing done today, I will be satisfied." Sound familiar? Regardless of if I am feeling under the weather or exhausted, I am constantly pushing myself to do "just one more thing." If I have to be honest, if someone else were pushing me to do "that one more thing," I would be extremely annoyed, even perturbed, so why do I do it to myself? When I begin to feel stress or anxiety, especially at work, I take a moment to think about all I have accomplished and remind myself to be kind to myself.

There are so many boundaries that can be identified to preserve the health of your personal and work life. Use your Personal Evaluation and Goal Attainment worksheets to reveal the boundaries needed to maintain that balance.

What are some boundaries that you can put in place to keep balance in your personal and work life?

THE P.R.O.F.I.T. COST PROCESS

When it comes to pricing a product, the traditional formula is straightforward. The wholesale cost of the product, or if you are creating the product, the cost to produce, such as labor, equipment, and materials, is determined. Then, a markup that will satisfy fixed costs as well as a profit is added. But what about additional costs outside of the cost to produce or sell your product or service? What about placing a monetary value on your expertise and creative outputs? There are many overlooked and unconsidered components that should be included to ensure overall business success when developing a pricing strategy.

Before explaining the P.R.O.F.I.T. Cost Process, I am going to set the stage with a business scenario. Let's imagine you have gotten your health and nutrition certification and are planning to open a healthy smoothie bar. You are well-educated on all aspects of health and nutrition, have attended many conferences, and have been a long-time contributor to your local health and fitness magazine. Healthy living is your passion, and although you are a newbie to the business world aspect of health and nutrition, you are an expert on the subject and have some pretty innovative, game-changing ideas. You have always dreamed of opening your own smoothie bar, but this shop will be like no other. Your concept is to educate your clients on their personal nutrition habits and offer personalized smoothies to meet their specific needs. Each ingredient option will have an informational card displayed that explains the benefits that the item can add to the customer's overall health. Once the patron customizes their smoothie, you will offer food pairing options for them to choose from, which will help to enhance their smoothie's health benefits for a complete, nutritious meal. Your shop will also have an informational library with various health and fitness books, and will host complementary nutrition seminars, giving your clients access to your professional recommendations on dieting and healthy lifestyle changes. Your business will take the hard work out of nutrition decisions and be a one-stop shop for learning balanced consumption habits and positive lifestyle changes. This is an establishment created by a health specialist *(you)* in which you will pass on your knowledge through a product and service offering at a fraction of the price that a personal nutritionist would charge. Sure, there are thousands of smoothie bars out there, but you are selling more than just a smoothie, you are selling total health using your expert knowledge and an overall heightened lifestyle experience. Your design and unique selling point are gold, but what about your pricing model?

THE P.R.O.F.I.T. COST PROCESS

In this section we will use the smoothie bar example to navigate the P.R.O.F.I.T Cost Process for determining the final sales price for your product or service. I use the P.R.O.F.I.T. Cost Process as a base for easily understanding costs, researching the market, budgeting to further my expertise, and assigning a competitive price to products and services.

This process will first take you through a basic understanding of direct production costs. This aspect may or may not be applicable to your business. The next step of this process is to review your rivals' pricing, or competition pricing; this challenges you to better understand your target market. The overt and fixed costs steps of the process are used to review the total costs associated with your business so that you can ensure every single tangible expense is accounted for in pricing your product or service. In the P.R.O.F.I.T. Cost Process, the next element is called *impact cost.* This cost is rarely evaluated in traditional pricing strategies, but is a very important component nevertheless, as it enables you to assign a value to your expertise. Once each of the first five areas of cost are determined, you add your total profit margin for a final product or service price.

P.   Production Cost

R.   Rival Benchmark

O.   Overt Costs

F.   Fixed Costs

I.   Impact Cost

T.   Total Profit Margin

Production Cost

production costs - costs directly associated with the manufacturing of a product or costs directly associated with conducting a service.

The Production cost is a component of the P.R.O.F.I.T. Cost Process that refers to the direct cost of producing goods or services. This includes the labor costs of employees on a production line painting a product, hair stylists performing a service, or a waiter serving a patron, to name a few examples.

Using our smoothie business example, we can examine the production costs associated with creating one smoothie by reviewing the cost breakdown of the ingredients, machinery, and labor needed to produce one smoothie. By the way, I have never run or operated a smoothie establishment and therefore, the following examples of cost are not derived from real-life scenarios and should not be used as a basis for conducting your own smoothie business.

After measuring out the ingredients used in each smoothie, we know that, on average that $0.75 worth of ingredients are needed to create one smoothie product. Merely pricing the materials *(ingredients)* needed to produce one unit *(smoothie)*is not enough to determine the overall production cost. Machinery and labor costs must also be included in the equation to derive a true cost per unit *(smoothie.)*

Next, we calculate the cost of using our high-powered, professional-grade blender. After making several test smoothies, we are able to determine that the average time for producing one smoothie is five minutes. Let's imagine that our blender will have 2,000 hours of operation time before needing to be replaced. In order to determine machinery costs, you will need to consider how much you originally paid for the blender, then divide that retail price by 120,000 minutes *(which is the equivalent to 2,000 hours)* and multiply that number by five.

$2,500 (machine cost) / 120,000 min (usage life)
= $0.02 per minute of usage

$0.02 x 5 min = $0.10 machine cost per smoothie

The outcome value will give you the machinery cost for five minutes of blender usage. Since the machine originally cost $2,500, your machine cost per smoothie would be $0.10.

When we add the machine cost to the material cost, we see that our cost to produce one smoothie is $0.85. But wait, you aren't finished yet.

$0.75 (material cost per smoothie) +
$0.10 (machine cost per smoothie) = $0.85

When creating a product, the wages of your staff who are making the product, directly contributing to the creation of your product, are considered part of the production cost. If you offer a service, the wages of your employees who are directly performing the service for your clients are also considered part of the production cost. Many question why labor is considered an indirect cost in non-service or non-production businesses and a direct cost in production operations. When running a production line or conducting a service, your staff's labor is considered a direct cost to the development of your product or service because they are physically involved in the creation process. Therefore, their labor cost must be included in your total unit cost.

In order to determine labor costs in the smoothie business example, you must ask the question, if a smoothie is made by one employee and takes five minutes to make, how much is that employee paid for those five minutes? You pay your employee $15 per hour, we can determine that each minute our employee works equals $0.25, which is $1.25 per smoothie.

$15 hr / 60 minutes = $0.25

$0.25 (labor per min) x 5 min =
$1.25 labor cost per smoothie

The labor cost per smoothie would then be added to our production cost equation to increase the cost of one smoothie to $2.10.

$0.75 (material cost) + $0.10 (machine cost)
+ $1.25 (labor cost) = $2.10 (production cost)

Now, let's take it one step further and say that you are wholesaling your smoothies to grocery stores. In this case, you would incur transportation costs, as you will need a delivery service to get your smoothies to the contracted grocery stores. Imagine that it costs $350 to deliver 2,000 smoothies. In this case, you divide $350 by 2,000 units to get a delivery cost of $0.18 per smoothie (rounded up.)

$350 delivery fee / 2,000 smoothies
per delivery = $0.18 delivery cost per smoothie

Once this additional cost is included in the production cost formula, you have a final cost of $2.28 per unit (smoothie.)

$0.75 (cost of materials) + $0.10 (machinery costs) + $1.25 (labor costs)
+ $0.18 (transportation) = $2.28 (cost per unit)

The production cost piece of the P.R.O.F.I.T. Cost Process helps you to determine your direct cost to produce one unit or service. As you will see there are other costs that should be factored into the equation.

Rival Benchmark

rival benchmark - evaluating your direct and indirect competitors'
product/service offerings and price ranges as a point of
reference for helping to create your own product/service
portfolio and price points.

When deciding on your pricing structure it is important to compare your business offerings and price points against your closest competition to determine where you fit into the market landscape and to be sure you are running a competitively lean operation. To do this, you must conduct a full competitive landscape analysis, which includes examining the pricing structure of your direct and indirect competition. Direct competitors would be those that offer the same product or service as your business, while indirect competition includes those that provide a product or service that could be considered a substitute for your offering.

In the smoothie bar example, a direct competitor to your business would be any smoothie bar located in your market. A general rule of thumb is to research all establishments within 50 miles of your business. While it seems unlikely that your customer would drive 50 miles to a competitor for a little bit less expensive smoothie, understanding the competitive pricing landscape within your metropolitan area will help you to understand what your target market perceives as an acceptable price to pay for your product category.

An indirect competitor to your smoothie bar would be any similar business model concept. Perhaps a build-your-own berry bowl shop that also provides clients with nutrition seminars is located 10 miles from your ideal location. True, they are not selling smoothies, but they are selling a healthy alternative substitute to your product and also offering nutrition workshops and seminars. Because they too provide a total health solution, your customer could view them as an alternative to visiting your shop. To ensure that your pricing strategy is well-rounded, you will need to investigate product offerings and price points from substitute businesses as well.

While innovation, unique creative concepts, and the value of your own expertise may allow you to push your pricing beyond the scale, conducting a Competitive Price Point Analysis by researching your direct and indirect competitors will help establish a baseline for setting your product/service pricing.

Competitive Price Point Analysis

Who are your direct competitors? What are their product or service price ranges?

_____

_____

Who are your indirect competitors? What are their product or service price ranges?

_____

_____

With the competitive research you have performed, create a pricing scale based solely on the research of your **direct competitors'** prices for the same offering.

List your direct competitors' lowest, middle, and highest price points.

_____

_____

With the competitive research you have performed, create a pricing scale based solely on the research of your **indirect competitors'** pricing for a similar offering.

List your indirect competitors' lowest, middle, and highest price points.

_____

_____

Overt Costs (Variable Costs)

overt costs - usually fluctuating costs, outside of production costs, which are overtly linked to non-production or service business operations, also referred to as <u>variable costs</u> in the business world.

For the sake of keeping my acronym of P.R.<u>O</u>.F.I.T. Cost Process intact, I have chosen to use the word *overt* to refer to a variable cost. For the sake of minimizing confusion among readers, I will use the widely recognized business term *variable costs* in place of overt costs throughout this discussion.

With the majority of the population using credit cards, the popularity of delivery services, fees charged when selling on social platforms, and additional costs rendered when selling a product through unconventional business methods, it is helpful to understand your variable costs when pricing your goods and services. While production costs are directly related to costs associated with *producing* an item or service, variable costs are dependent upon and fluctuate with, sales operations. For example, credit card fees. Not everyone pays with a credit card when making a purchase, but transactions that are completed with a credit card will incur a fee. Other varying costs may include commissions, shopping bags, packaging supplies, and for job positions outside of direct production or service activities, labor costs.

Let's take a minute to discuss labor costs that are considered variable costs. When running a women's clothing store, unless you are physically making garments in-house, your labor costs will not be assigned as a production cost because you are not running a production operation. In this instance, labor costs will be committed to the variable cost category. While these costs may seem like fixed costs because they exist regardless of whether the shop makes a sale, they are actually variable costs. If store sales slump, then the boutique owner may choose to reduce employee hours to save on labor costs. On the other hand, if the business is cycling into a seasonal high, the store owner may hire additional employees to cover the influx of customers, which in turn, increases labor costs. Wage raises, bonuses, and economic changes can also shift overall labor costs. Therefore, since labor costs can vary based on operational needs, it is considered a variable cost.

In our smoothie bar example, in addition to production costs, you will incur several types of variable costs, such as credit card processing fees, take-out bags, and employee wages, to name a few. I know what you are thinking, "But we included labor costs for making the smoothie in the production section." The smoothie bar example is unique in that we produce our product and also sell the product in a retail setting. Suppose we did not sell one smoothie on Monday, but we had two employees present. The labor cost will still exist regardless of whether there is a sale. In business settings in which you make a product in-house and then sell that product, I advise you to track labor costs in both the production of the product and in the overt cost category. This will help you to keep track of the true cost per unit, while also enabling you to make business decisions based on labor needs and affordability. In retail operations in which you do not make a product in-house or perform a paid service, you may disregard the production cost portion of the P.R.O.F.I.T. Cost Process.

When it comes to applying the variable costs to your overall product or service price, I recommend averaging these costs quarterly, year over year, based on average units or services sold, and then adding these costs to your wholesale product cost, service cost, or production cost.

$2,000 (variable cost previous year - Q1)/ 2,500 (units sold previous year - Q1) = $0.80 (variable cost per unit)

$2.10 (cost per unit) + $0.80 (variable cost) = $2.90 per smoothie

Keep in mind, that since variable costs fluctuate based on sales, you will need to keep close tabs on the percentage increase or decrease in sales per quarter and adjust your equation accordingly. Instead of raising or lowering prices quarterly, understand the breakdown of your variable costs so that you can, alternatively, make decisions on where to cut costs to maintain profits while keeping your prices steady.

Fixed Costs

fixed costs - costs that remain constant and are not directly influenced by production or sales activities.

Fixed costs are expenses that are incurred whether your business is open or closed. In other words, if you decide to close your shop on Sundays, you will still be responsible for rent, utility bills, and insurance. Since your fixed costs do not generally fluctuate, other than your utility bill, these costs can be assessed annually instead of quarterly. I recommend dividing your total annual fixed cost by the number of products or services that you plan to sell in a year, and then apply that dollar amount to your product cost.

For our equation below, we will imagine that our annual fixed cost is $20,000 and that we plan to sell 15,000 smoothies this year.

$$\$20,000 \text{ (annual fixed cost)} / 15,000 \text{ (annual units sold)}$$
$$= \$1.33 \text{ (fixed cost per unit)}$$

$$\$2.10 \text{ (production cost)} + \$0.80 \text{ (variable costs)} + \$1.33 \text{ (fixed costs)}$$
$$= \$4.23 \text{ (unit cost)}$$

Fully understanding the production, overt, and fixed costs associated with conducting business will help you as an unconventional entrepreneur determine how much you need to sell per month in order to cover overhead and break even. Now, but what about turning a profit?

Impact Cost

impact - the effect or influence of one person, thing, or action on another. (Oxford Lexico)

impact cost - the cost assigned to your "influence" or expertise, which can be invested into furthering your skill set or used to reimburse yourself for work you have already put into building your expertise.

There is one very important cost that is often missed or undervalued by many entrepreneurs, and that is the cost of your expertise. A unique, creative concept linked to a trusted expert renders a product or service that is sure to be worth more in the consumer's eyes. So how do you monetize that worth? This is a question that we all ask ourselves when launching a business. Sadly, most of us think we are worth far less than we actually are due to lack of confidence, or "the fear of putting ourselves out there."

I remember when I started blogging. I was confident in my expertise on the topics that I shared, but always questioned what others would think. Were my makeup tutorial videos professional enough? Was my content interesting? Was I being judged? We fear that others will not see value in our offering which leads us to undervalue ourselves. Often we have an idea of how we would like to price our offerings, but when push comes to shove, fear drives us to accept a monetary value that is far less than what we are worth. When you are not solid in your understanding of what you are worth, you may develop unhealthy business practices, such as underselling or haggling, which ultimately leads to being overworked and underpaid.

So, what makes you "worth it" to the consumer? How can you build the internal confidence needed to recognize your worth? While an expert with ten years in an industry would generally be paid much more than someone who has been in the game for just a few months, consumers place high value on public recognition, knowledge, novelty, and unique ideas. If you position yourself to become a familiar face in your market, have the knowledge and training to back yourself up, and have a creative concept that people are attracted to, you will not only build the internal confidence needed, but will have accrued value in the eyes of your target market. Voilà! Now that you have the internal confidence to ask for what you are worth and have built trust within your target market base, you are ready to price your products or services at a premium.

◆ ◆ ◆

Unconventional Wisdom
Be more than just a business, be the expert.

◆ ◆ ◆

People hire experts when they don't know how to do something or need professional guidance beyond their knowledge. Many professionals are conditioned to charge for their time, but becoming an expert requires more than just an investment of time and money. Becoming an expert requires mastery, skill, a steadfast mindset, and perseverance. It's not an easy task. To remain an industry expert, an unconventional entrepreneur must constantly pursue and invest in new knowledge and improve upon their skill set. For this reason, we should consider more than the traditional practice of charging by the hour. Instead, the unconventional entrepreneur should include a small premium for their knowledge, mastery, and the work that they have put into their craft. This premium will enable the entrepreneur to further their knowledge and expertise in the future. For example, in my business, I do not have an hourly rate. Sure, if I take on speaking engagements, I must evaluate the time required such as how many days I am needed to speak, the location of the engagement, the number of event appearances I must make, and my annual salary, but after these costs are considered, I then adjust my price for the speaking engagement to consider my impact cost and profit margin.

Many entrepreneurs mistakenly assume that their annual salary is their profit. Like employees, the business owner's annual salary should be factored into the pricing process as part of the overall labor costs. I must admit, I incorrectly based my pricing strategy on this understanding for years. In several instances, when sales were tight, I unexpectedly came up short, with no extra funds budgeted for business or personal growth. To ensure funds are available for future business and personal growth, you must include your annual salary into your labor cost and apply an impact cost and a profit margin on top of your production, overt, and fixed costs.

While there is no real formula for determining this up charge, I recommend taking a look at your competitive pricing scale and valuing yourself accordingly. For example, let's imagine that the competitive price range for a smoothie, or substitute, in your market is between $7.00 and $10.00. We have calculated your unit cost to be $4.23. If you marked your product up 50%, your final price per smoothie would be $8.46. You are within the competitive price range. Perhaps you will set your impact cost at $0.15 per smoothie, which brings your final unit price to $8.61. You are still within your competitive price range, but now you are being compensated for your expertise. If you sell 15,000 smoothies for the entire year, you then have $2,250 in your impact cost account, which you can use to further your health and nutritional certifications or as compensation for the time you have already spent acquiring and building your expertise. It may seem silly to consider your impact cost while pricing your product. Remember, however, that you need superior knowledge to remain competitive as the leading industry expert. In order to remain ahead of the game, build a strategy that plans for future investments in personal growth.

Total Profit Margin

profit - obtain a financial advantage or benefit, especially from an investment. (Oxford Lexico)

total profit margin - the percentage of a sale that is considered profit.

Profit is a financial gain made from a monetary or time investment. Since an investment is always considered a risk, big or small, the profit gained from said investment is your reward for taking that risk. To ensure a healthy profit is returned from the sale of each individual product or service, a profit margin percentage must be assigned to the product. The total profit margin is the percentage of a sale that is returned as profit. Many business owners use their profits to reinvest in business growth, inventory expansion, employee salary raises, etc.

When I owned The Ivory Closet, I attributed 15% of every sale to my fixed overhead and 30% to my overt costs, which left 55% of every sale, after my break-even point, allocated to my impact cost and profit margin. Every market is different. To better understand profit margins within your industry and determine a healthy markup for your company, turn to Google or consult a fellow business owner with a similar shop in a non-competing market.

The P.R.O.F.I.T. Cost Process establishes a baseline blueprint for pricing and acts as a guide when making important decisions that may influence pricing. If you know the exact breakdown of each component, you can easily gain insight into over-or-under expenditures and identify opportunities for improvement. Keep in mind that not all businesses are equal. Should you have a more complex business idea that requires additional levels to your pricing strategy, the P.R.O.F.I.T. Cost Process is a starting point that can be built upon.

OMNICHANNEL FOR SMALL BUSINESS

Many entrepreneurs fail to realize the effects of rapid technological change on the business landscape. With email newsletters, social media channels, the popularity of pop-up shops, blogs, mobile apps, e-commerce shops, same-day delivery services, review services, virtual reality shops, chat boxes, and more, a brand can now be present at every touch point of the customer journey.

omnichannel - multichannel approach to sales that seeks to provide customers with a seamless shopping experience, whether they're shopping online from a desktop or mobile device, by telephone, or in a brick-and-mortar store.

An omnichannel strategy is a strategy in which you create a consistent, seamless brand experience that allows the customer to easily interact with your brand through mediums that best suit their needs. In the past, this omnichannel experience was only available to big box brands with deep pockets; however, new integrative technologies and innovative business solutions for entrepreneurs enable small businesses to compete using a holistic omnichannel strategy. This approach aims to provide solutions for the customer at every touch point in their journey with your brand.

So how does an unconventional entrepreneur embrace the omnichannel strategy? Let's take a step back and look in depth at the generations in the U.S. and their values. There are five living generations active in the workforce and markets today: the Silent Generation, Baby Boomers, Generation X, Millennials, and Generation Z. Each of these generations have very different wants, needs, and values that can all be satisfied via an ominchannel strategy. Research from Business Clan gives us further insight into each generation.

The Silent Generation is made up of those born between 1928 and 1945, the years that span from the beginning of the Great Depression to the end of WWII. Due to the era of this generation, they tend to be very thrifty, attracted to traditional values, and appreciate a practical approach to advertising. They are extremely loyal in their lifestyle and consumption habits, many being employed at one company their entire life and repeatedly choosing the same brands in their purchase decisions. This group is considered the least technologically savvy of the five generations; however, they have embraced online purchasing for purposes of convenience.

Those born between 1946 and 1964 are considered Baby Boomers. This generation prefers gathering their information through traditional print means, but because this medium for marketing and information delivery is on a rapid decline, they have been forced to adapt to the twenty-first century's means of communication. When it comes to digital use, Baby Boomers are known to spend more time on a desktop computer rather than a mobile device. Most use social platforms purely for communication purposes, which means they are unlikely to respond to a hard-sell social ad. Search engine marketing, however, would be a great strategy when targeting this group, as more Boomers are turning to the internet when seeking information. While comfortable with text messaging, research by Business Clan has found that 95% of Baby Boomers prefer email to instant messaging when it comes to digital communication. This generation appreciates face-to-face and phone communication with real people, as opposed to chatbots. Due to learning curves often associated with technology and the propensity for choosing traditional communication methods, Baby Boomers prefer the simplest uses of technology.

Born between 1965 and 1980 are the members of Generation X. Generation X has fully embraced digital media; however, they are known to be time-poor, often making them too busy to leisurely explore the digital world. While this group still prefers broadcast TV as their main source of entertainment, when it comes to traditional print media versus digital press, they prefer digital news outlets and social media platforms, such as Facebook, as their sources for obtaining news information and socializing. They appreciate visually engaging content but want to see the practical use of the products that have piqued their interest. This generation places a high value on reviews and is more likely to research a product or service before making a purchase decision. When it comes to conversion, roughly half of Gen X'ers are motivated through the use of discounts and coupons, and almost all are members of at least one brand loyalty program. This group also straddles the line of traditional and digital consumption patterns when purchasing, wanting complete mobile integration across every stage of the process, whether in-store or at home.

Tech-savvy Millennials, or the Y2K generation, were born between 1981 and 1996. Millennials tend to make ethical buying decisions as they are very socially conscious and strive to make a difference in the world through the use of their voice and buying behavior. Research has shown that 70% of Millennials will spend more with brands that support causes that they believe in. This group craves authenticity, which leads them to reject, and even distrust, traditional marketing strategies. Like Gen X, Millennials are influenced by loyalty programs and will participate in comparison research before making a purchase. They want to be part of the conversation or creative process, and therefore, will spend a lot of time on social platforms and mobile devices, for reasons beyond pure social fulfillment. Millennials often establish attitudes towards a brand and brand preferences through influencers and advocates often sought out on Facebook, Instagram, and almost every other leading social platform invented during their era. Due to the volatile nature of the market environment to which they have grown accustomed, Millennials seek a heightened experience to traditional forms of retail, entertainment, and overall consumption. This generation has experienced unprecedented technological and digital advances, which have made them adaptable and even welcoming, to new, market-disrupting digital products and services, such as Amazon Prime and Netflix.

While Generation Z is not the final living generation, it is the youngest working generation, born between the years 1996 to 2012. Because this generation is inundated with so many sources for digital access, bouncing between tablets, laptops, mobile devices, gaming consoles, and TV, their attention span is very short, which means any attempt at engagement with this audience must be unique. It is important to be relevant, brief, and to the point with this group. Unlike Baby Boomers, who are more familiar with mass industrialization, this generation is accustomed to tailor-made experiences and personalized services. While quality trumps brand loyalty with Gen. Z, meaningful engagements are still highly valued. Generation Z are communicators, openly speaking their opinions and offering transparent feedback. Due to their heightened demand for transparency and attraction to attainable lifestyles through relatable sources, like Millennials, Gen Z'ers have further given rise to the influencer celebrity. They are much more likely to place their favorite YouTube star on a pedestal over an A-list star. Also, like Millennials, this generation makes ethical buying choices and will align their purchase decisions with brands that support their social ideals.

So why did we just do a mini review of each working generation? As you can see, while all groups share values, they differ drastically in their preferences and consumption methods. An unconventional entrepreneur understands that while you can't be everything to everyone, an omnichannel experience can be used to mend the gaps so that you may appeal to more than one generational demographic and create a seamless brand experience across every customer touch point based on generational preferences.

For example, the Silent Generation has embraced digital commerce for convenience purposes. If you plan to sell to this demographic, you will want to be sure to offer delivery services in addition to e-commerce and brick and mortar environment, so that you can bring the experience of your business to them. On the other hand, Baby Boomers use digital platforms a little more regularly than the Silent Generation, not intentionally for purchasing, but rather for social communications. Research reveals that this group does not like to be sold to, and that they use Facebook over any other social platform. If this is one of your target demographics your business should provide useful information and content that offers solutions via Facebook, instead of hard-sell ads, to create buzz and increase engagement with your brand. Because research has shown that Baby Boomers use the internet for information gathering, a strategy that positions your brand in search engines would further the brand experience across platforms. Research has also revealed that this group prefers email over direct messaging, therefore an email newsletter with consistent brand visuals will further build your business by bringing the brand experience straight to your customer's inbox. Remember, the Baby Boomer generation prefers a desktop computer for digital use. Make sure your e-commerce website and all emails are responsive, which means that they will display correctly on both a desktop and mobile device.

Since we know Generation X uses social platforms to remain social, since they have little to no time to be physically present in social settings, and they rely heavily on reviews before making a purchase decision if this is your target demographic you will want to make sure that reviews of your product or service are present on your social platforms, websites, third-party platforms *(Google Reviews or Yelp,)* blogs, and influencer platforms. Encourage images in these reviews so that text can be tied to a visual component for further brand exposure. Due to the time constraints of this group, make sure your conversion efforts, information delivery, and brand experience are streamlined and practical, yet memorable and appealing.

Millennials want to be a part of the action, creators of their environment, and disrupters for change. This motive is evident in their social platform usage and consumption habits. Since this group is more likely to favor products that donate to a cause that they believe in, cause-based marketing should be part of your strategy. What cause is near and dear to your and your customer's heart? Align your business and company culture with a philanthropic cause. Set up tables at non-profit events or host a charitable event in-house. Dedicate an area on your website, social platforms, and in-store to share information on your supported cause. Donate a portion of the sales of one of your products or overall sales to a cause. These efforts will not only appeal to Millennials but will strengthen the omnichannel experience by expanding your brand into new environments.

As you can see, there are many opportunities to streamline your ominchannel strategy through generational overlap. Generation Z, like Millennials, want to be leaders for change and will respond positively to cause-based marketing. We know Gen Z relies on a multitude of social platforms for communicating, information gathering, product or service research, and purchasing, therefore, you will be able to streamline your brand experience and create the ultimate omnichannel by leveraging your marketing and branding efforts across a multitude of marketing mediums.

From this review of the characteristics of different generations, it is apparent that as we get closer to the present-day generations, technology usage grows exponentially, attention spans shorten, and customized experiences are critical for competing against larger corporate brands. While the omnichannel strategy was not originally introduced as a solution for marketing across generational gaps, a solid omnichannel experience will serve to satisfy many audiences.

The omnichannel is a strategy that has been recognized for quite some time as the ultimate brand strategy but hasn't been available to small businesses due to the costs involved with platform integration. However, with small businesses on the rise, there has been increasing demand for total package systems that satisfy multichannel integrations and allow for an omnichannel strategy among small businesses at little to no extra cost. This has made it easier than ever for a small business to capitalize on the omnichannel strategy and bring its brand experience directly to the customer.

◆◆◆

Unconventional Wisdom
Keep the omnichannel top of mind.

◆◆◆

The perfect ominchannel strategy is one in which the customer recognizes your brand through experience without ever having to see the logo. Remember the 4 Senses Strategy? The scent, color scheme, voice, and quality of your brand all play a part in the total experience. How will you deliver this experience at every customer touch point? Let's imagine a marketing strategy absent your brand logo. Would your customer still recognize your brand? Of course, you would never actually leave your brand name and logo out of your marketing materials, but in order to ensure an iron-clad omnichannel experience, this is a great approach for brainstorming. As I mentioned earlier, I owned a women's clothing store for more than seven years before selling the business. To help get your creative juices flowing, I will share my omnichannel blueprint for my women's clothing store.

Incorporating the 4 Senses Strategy in a Brick-and-Mortar Store

As you may recall, beyond the color scheme, décor, and quality products in my store, I chose a brand scent that would flow throughout the store via a scent machine. Not only was this scent instantly recognizable upon entering the store, but it also allowed me to continue the brand experience outside of my shop setting. When the customer got home with their purchase, the shop scent permeated through their home as they removed their goods from their shopping bag. Also, when hosting pop-up shops or attending women's shopping shows, I was able to scent the sales area with my brand fragrance, which was instantly recognized by customers who frequented the shop. It also made the perfect introduction for those who were new to my brand.

A Shop App for Loyal Clients

Traditionally, custom apps were super expensive and could only be obtained by big brands, but in the last few years, many development companies have begun to create custom apps at an extremely affordable price for small businesses. Having a loyalty app for your business adds an additional source for direct contact with your customer through their mobile device. I called my mobile app the Style Club. Every client who had downloaded the app would get VIP exclusive access to Secret Stash notifications, insider knowledge on new brands that would be coming into the shop, and even the opportunity to vote on products that they wanted to see in store. This app allowed them to have a voice and to be part of an exclusive community.

Consistent Branded Emails

Every Tuesday I sent out a notification within the shop app and a "Secret Stash" email. The exclusive notification and email, sent only to Style Club members, shared heavily discounted, upcoming new arrivals for early access and pre-purchase. This allowed me to test for product popularity while providing the customer with a unique insider opportunity. I combined the style app and email marketing with an in-store experience by hosting a weekly Stash Hour, where Style Club clients could take advantage of a limited-time discount on merchandise straight out of the box. The Secret Stash sales were an instant hit and brought many new customers. Because Secret Stash was unique to The Ivory Closet and the sale could be experienced across several platforms, it was a great addition to my omnichannel strategy. This is an extreme example of how I used email to propel my strategy. An email that is beautifully designed to match your brand colors and tone is a simple, yet powerful start.

Loyalty Program

Want to show customer appreciation while making your client feel like they are part of the family? Implement a unique loyalty program. Many brands begin by offering discounts in their loyalty program; however, customers are becoming desensitized to discount programs and therefore, require more in exchange for their loyalty. A traditional loyalty program is designed to reward customers who have already experienced your brand with some sort of discount or money savings. The omnichannel loyalty program not only rewards spending behavior but also cultivates loyalty by creating an emotional and connected experience in which the client is inclined to share their encounter with your brand. The customer lifetime value in an omnichannel loyalty program is not only calculated by the amount of money that the customer spends with your business, but also by the exposure that they provide for your brand.

For The Ivory Closet, I created a three-tier loyalty program that offered different discounts, events, and experiences for clients depending on their level of loyalty. For example, the first tier, or my "fashionistas," would get access to private store events, customer-only sales, and "closet cash" for dollar-off discounts on their purchases.

These clients were also rewarded when they left a review of our shop on Google or Facebook and when tagging photos of themselves in-store or out and about while styled in Ivory Closet fashion. Tier two, or "trend mavens," received everything in tier one with an added bonus of gifts with purchase when they met spending thresholds along with invites to in-store and digital private shopping events. Tier three, or our "style icons," could take advantage of everything offered in tiers one and two, but also received private personal shopping experiences, extended shopping hours, a standing discount on every purchase made with our shop and invites to our annual charity fashion show.

Beacon Technology

As you know by now, the goal of the omnichannel strategy is to integrate the business brand into the customer's everyday life by bringing the enterprise to them. Early on, Amazon recognized the value of brand/lifestyle integration and pioneered beacon technology through their press-to-order, Dash program. Amazon offered Dash order buttons for everyday household items so when their customer was in need of, toilet paper, for example, they just pressed the Amazon Dash button and toilet paper would arrive at their door. Another example of beacon technology at its finest is Target's "target run" function within the Target app. Customers who have downloaded the app, have Bluetooth turned on, and are in a "target run" Target location, will receive product recommendations based on the department they are shopping within the store. Both examples are from large corporations; however, beacon technology is accessible to small businesses as well. When I owned The Ivory Closet, I partnered with a media company to implement beacon technology for notifying current clients and potential customers via text of our weekly specials or exclusive offers when they physically entered my shop's geo location. Of course, to comply with digital privacy policies, these customers signed up for the notifications via my business or the media company that offered the beacon technology.

Interactive Experiences

Another great way to stay connected with your target demographic outside of your business location is through event participation. While a pop-up shop allows you to conduct business in different markets and meets the strategy of bringing your business straight to the customer, an atmosphere designed merely to promote sales is all too predictable. Focus on aligning your business with an event that complements your brand while creating interactive, memorable experiences for potential clients who are attending the event. For example, a cosmetic brand participating in a women's beauty event can sponsor a "Booze and Brow Hour," during which the cosmetic line offers complimentary champagne and five-minute brow makeovers. Imagine you are attending a local women's shopping event. You have had fun checking out the booths, demonstrations, and other activities provided. At four o'clock, two hours before the event concludes for the day, someone gets on the PA system and announces that Booze and Brow hour is taking place in booth number 25. You decide that you could use a glass of champagne and now that you think of it, you have always struggled with figuring out a brow shape that best fits your facial frame. When you get to booth 25, the music is popping, an extraordinary scent permeates the air, the shabby chic decor has you feeling like you have stepped back into a 1950s pink and posh beauty salon, and there are a host of people, some who work for the cosmetic line and others who have just gotten their free service, all with perfect brows. The experience not only educates the client but excites the senses at the same time. Of course, there is product on hand should a customer want to purchase their perfect brow kit or your signature scented candles, but the product is not overly displayed and certainly not pushed by the company representatives. This event is about creating a memorable experience and gaining brand exposure.

Creating interactive experiences outside of my boutique proved to be a wildly successful strategy for my business. Twice a year I set up shop at local women's shows by creating a mini makeover event in which I offered free styling services and makeup refreshes. My customers loved learning about the cuts and fabrics that fit their body type, color palettes that matched their complexion and feeling pampered overall. Of course, I hoped for sales at these events, but this truly was not the primary goal. By providing a memorable brand interaction that would encourage *brand experience cohesion* for my audience, I could evoke a positive emotional attachment to my brand and create higher chances of brand recall, both resulting in the potential for future sales.

Social Media and Blog

By now, I think it is clear how social media fits into the omnichannel experience. Blogs combined with social platforms can be used to showcase your expertise and rapidly build trust in your business. Blogs aren't just for bloggers and influencers, they are great sources for companies to grow online traffic, gather leads, convert new customers, engage with current customers, showcase expertise, build demand for their product or service, and gain continuous SEO benefits from content long after publishing. Along with all these wonderful benefits, a company's blog is the perfect strategy for building an omnichannel experience because the content can be shared across multiple platforms.

I started my blog as a way to share trendy fashion updates, makeup tutorials, and wardrobe tips. Of course, I used products that I carried in my store in my blog content, but the overall goal was to attract potential customers, build expertise, and further brand exposure. Instead of pushing sales, I kept my content informationally focused so that I could appeal to a target demographic who rejected traditional sales tactics. To cross-promote platforms, I included buttons on my blog which directed readers to my social sites and online shop. Likewise, in order to drive traffic to the blog, I shared my blog content in weekly newsletters and on social media. This encouraged movement and interaction between the company blog, social platforms, and email and helped to create a consistent, seamless brand experience and further brand exposure.

Retargeting Marketing

Most people who visit your website for the first time and do not convert via subscribing to a newsletter or making a purchase, are less likely to return to your site without being reminded of your brand. After all, before a person will shell out their cash, they want to feel like they know and trust your business. Therefore, retargeting is essential for the omnichannel strategy. Retargeting platforms help to keep your brand top of mind by tracking customers who have visited your website, and then remarketing to them with relevant visual or textual content on other websites that they visit. This adds to your omnichannel strategy by offering additional exposure to your brand across several platforms.

Many companies successfully convert their audience by using a product discount retargeting strategy. I found that by creating appealing and engaging brand content absent a sales push, yet specific to the target demographic's location was effective in increasing brand recognition and brand recall. At The Ivory Closet, we carried a line of area-code-specific baseball caps. After researching my website's audience demographic via Google Analytics, I learned that Memphis, Nashville, and Atlanta were the top cities from which my website visitors originated. I decided to do a photoshoot with models wearing our area code baseball caps to produce location-specific content. At the bottom of each area code-specific image, I simply included our company logo. Then, I uploaded the images to a retargeting platform and set the retargeting action to show an area-code-specific image to those who live in that area-code and have visited our company website. For example, someone from Atlanta who has visited our website would be served an ad on Facebook that shows our models wearing the Atlanta area code baseball caps.

Influencer Marketing

Influencer marketing is unique in that it is a form of user-generated content. User-generated content is any content created from a source other than the brand, and which is considered to be unbiased with a heightened level of authenticity. In this type of marketing, a brand will send their product to an influencer. If the influencer likes the product, they may feel compelled to share their experience with their audience. For many influencers, reviewing products and services is a full-time job. Therefore, there are usually costs associated with influencer partnerships. When working with an influencer on any capacity, trade or paid, the Federal Trade Commission requires a disclosure statement be present in the content to prevent deceptive ads. This disclosure, in most cases, does not deter the audience from trusting the influencer's recommendations. According to Digital Marketing Institute, the influencer marketing industry is expected to exceed $13 billion by the end of 2022 with 49% of consumers depending on product or service suggestions given by influencers.

The loyalty that an influencer establishes with their following can be very strong and has given rise to this new form of marketing. Not only can an influencer recommendation instill favoritism towards a brand, it makes for great marketing content for the brand to share on their own digital platforms.

I established a very robust influencer program when running The Ivory Closet. Every month we would send "try on haul" products to 12 influencers whose audiences aligned with our target demographic. The influencers' audiences were continuously exposed to our brand. We positioned these influencers to be The Ivory Closet fashion experts and with their permission would use their user-generated content in our email newsletters, on our website, on our social platforms, and even in point-of-sale displays throughout the store. Because our current customers became familiar with the influencers via our marketing strategy, they were always extra excited to attend in-store events when our influencer fashionistas were present. Many of our influencers had overlapping audiences, which meant that our brand was being shared to many people through multiple influencer platforms. Including influencer marketing in our omnichannel strategy provided an additional, more authentic avenue for building brand loyalty and trust.

As you can see, a lot of work and thought goes into a branded omnichannel strategy, and while the rewards are worth it, the task can be very time-consuming and strenuous. Many begin on their business journey as a one-woman or one-man show, and quickly become overwhelmed with all the moving parts. That's why having a network of like-minded unconventional entrepreneurs is essential for continuous innovation within your business. It takes a village.

IT TAKES A VILLAGE

Consulting with other entrepreneurs in your market not only helps you to build a network of like-minded people to support your business efforts, but it also helps to increase your chances of business success through an exchange of ideas. Do you pigeonhole yourself by operating in a bubble, limited to your own thoughts and business concepts? When you do this, you close yourself off from the mentorship of other unconventional entrepreneurs who may be more knowledgeable about industry trends and current opportunities within the market.

Because I failed to realize the value in networking, my first few months in business were a disaster. I had concrete ideas on how I would run my business, from the products that I wanted to offer and inventory management processes, to marketing strategies and financial budgets. I thought I knew it all. The only problem was, I had never spent any appreciable time working in a clothing store, other than a two-month seasonal stint at American Eagle during the summer before college. I was under the impression that because I had earned my bachelor's degree in business and worked six years in corporate, I knew it all. I am literally chuckling at the thought of it right now. While I was ultimately successful in my first year of business, the start was nearly a disaster.

When it came to stocking my shop, I had no idea that a market existed for boutiques to purchase inventory, so I resorted to online wholesale sites. That shows you how little I knew. I had never touched or examined any clothing I was going to sell before my first shipment of worth more than $6,000 arrived. That is not enough to fill a 1000 square-foot store by the way. I learned that the hard way, too. Thankfully the clothing was of great quality but the fit on at least a third of my inventory was terrible. You know, when you pick up a medium, but it fits like an extra, extra small?

Much to my surprise, I sold through half of my stock on opening night. However, my excitement was short lived when I realized the inventory management process I had adopted was impossible to execute. The majority of boutique clothing ships from California. My shop was located in Memphis, TN. It takes a minimum of five business days from the time my clothing order was packaged to arrive at my shop. Unfortunately, after my grand opening party, I had a shop that was barely half-stocked with no back up inventory to put on the sales floor. Not a great first impression for new customers.

I found myself hanging by a thread. After shipments arrived, sales would go up, but no matter how hard I tried, I couldn't get the reorder process to work for me so that my store would remain stocked at all times. Cash would come in, inventory would dwindle, I'd spend cash on new inventory, and while I waited on shipments to arrive, cash was stagnant because I had nothing for customers to purchase.

I knew that if I couldn't keep my store stocked, maintain a healthy cash flow, and invest in some sort of marketing, I was doomed. I needed to figure out something fast. Scouring the pages of Google to find a solution wasn't cutting it. Of course, the thought had crossed my mind to reach out to another boutique owner for advice, but I knew I was their competition and didn't want them to think I was trying to steal their ideas. Even worse, I was ashamed because I had finally realized how little I knew about the industry. What would they think of me? They had probably poured their everything into their business and here I come, waltzing in, thinking it looks so easy while actually knowing nothing. I didn't even do my research. I would be annoyed with me too. What a rude awakening!

After months of carrying on this way, it dawned on me. There had to be associations out there for retail entrepreneurs to share best practices and ideas. I began researching and was able to find several organizations that looked like they could provide me some mentorship. Joining these support groups turned everything around for me. Not only did I become educated on how to properly manage my inventory and cash flow, but I learned all about unique, low-cost marketing strategies for boutique owners and where to shop for top brands to stock my store. In an instant, I had all the answers. I was so blown away by the value of these entrepreneurial groups that I set up a local networking group for non-competing, female business owners in Memphis so that we could band together to brainstorm business opportunities within our community for shared success.

Building a network of other successful business owners can provide so many benefits to your business. You will learn about competitor strategies, professional improvement, customer acquisition through shared events, novel sales techniques, business leads, trend identification, and most importantly, you get a different perspective through mentorship.

When building your village don't limit yourself to just one group for mentorship. Participate in many different business associations. You will discover that ideas are different among groups and by learning from entrepreneurs within your industry as well as those in similar industries, you will be better equipped to develop creative and innovative concepts that will advance your business.

Paper is Not Dead

I know this may come as a surprise to the unconventional entrepreneur who may think that anything on paper is dead, but up I can use paper to make a statement these days. When networking be sure to have to have a show-stopping business card. I can't tell you how many times someone has paused to admire my business card when I hand it to them. First, I believe it to be because the sheer act of handing someone a business card in this day and age takes the receiver off guard. Many young business owners do not carry business cards anymore. Second, I have invested in a high-quality business card design that is instantly memorable through touch. The card stock is heavy with a silky matte finish, it includes an image of myself with my brand logo, and on top of the expected details, such as my email and phone number, I have included a few fun facts about my brand. I know what you are thinking. A bit superficial, right? I felt the same way too when I was given this advice, but the business card must be an extension of you.

The person who takes your business card will often put it in their wallet or briefcase only to come across it again late. If your card includes your photo that person can quickly associate a face with your business and remember the exchange that they had with you earlier. Also, by investing in a top-quality paper and finish you are giving your card and business a sense of value. It may seem peculiar, but personally, I have kept business cards for the mere fact that they felt and looked too appealing to throw away. How could I trash this smooth, velvety, weighted business card with a fantastic portrait of the nice girl that I met last week at a women's luncheon? Some weird sense of loyalty that the card instills. Maybe that will make for a future research project.

In addition to a business card, you should always keep a portfolio piece on hand. A portfolio is similar to a resume or as it's referred to in the marketing industry, a media kit. This is a one-page, printed front and back, piece that includes your company logo, business details, statistics that may support your successes, accolades from your clients, a list of reputable companies that you have partnered with, and appealing visuals. Much like your business card, the paper and image quality matter. I have found enclosing it in a high-quality envelope with some sort of seal also adds allure. I keep several copies of my portfolio with me when I attend important conferences or events at which potential clients may be present. After having a conversation with someone who may be interested in working together or partnering on a mutually beneficial project, I offer up one of my envelopes, which also includes a business card, and set a time to follow up later on our conversation.

These are just two examples of how you can wow the people you meet while networking with a tangible item that represents an extension of you and your brand. I also like to send thank-you cards in the mail after an important, first-time meeting or invite to an event. A large part of networking is about making a positive gesture for a memorable first impression.

Maintain a Contact List

In a previous chapter, you listed groups that you would be interested in joining. After attending group meetings and networking events, be sure to upload all of your contacts into some sort of spreadsheet or database. Over the past 12 years of being in business for myself, I have built several contact lists. I have a list of brands that I have contracted with, local business contacts for event partnerships, other influencers for mutual collaborations, and peers from support groups. At the beginning of every year, I update my lists and also send a Happy New Year email to all of my contacts as a simple hello and to ensure the line of communication remains open.

Building a Village

Now is the time to get started on building your village. As I talked about in my previous story, networking throughout the business planning phase, well in advance of launching your business, will help you to better strategize and align your brand for introduction into the market. It is often the case when starting off in the business arena, a lack of know-how and capital can set you back before you start. Tap into thriving networks within your industry to get access to resources and information, as well as open the doors for opportunities that may not present themselves otherwise.

Strategic networking can help you find future employees, investors, customers, and even develop long-term, win-win partnerships for mutual growth and success. When you link up with a like-minded business whose goods and services are complementary to your own, both of you in the partnership will get mutually beneficial, exclusive access to resources that neither of you would have had otherwise. For example, recently I partnered with American Heart Association. One day, AHA reached out to me and asked about promoting some of their annual events on my social platforms. I have always wanted to make a meaningful difference with my work and thought this was the perfect opportunity to do so. We scheduled a meeting and began to brainstorm. Knowing that my blog is my full-time job, the AHA representative asked what I would want in exchange for the partnership. I really just wanted to make a difference and told them I would be happy to promote, support, and attend any of their events to help get the word out. During our second meeting, the American Heart Association representatives expressed their desire for our relationship to be mutually beneficial. They asked, "Was their anything they could do to help promote my business in exchange for my time?" After some thought, it dawned on me. The American Heart Association has a very large database here in Tennessee. My business profits are often tied to engagement measures from my social accounts and the number of active blog email newsletter subscribers. I thought, perhaps I could host the annual AHA women's luncheon fashion show, post about their philanthropic events throughout the year, and send an awareness email during February's heart month, in exchange for audience visibility. It was the perfect win-win scenario. Emceeing their fashion show provided my brand with exposure to over 300 women in the Memphis area. Hosting a ticket giveaway on my Instagram that was shared on AHA's social page where entrants were required to follow both AHA and my Instagram, helped with follower growth and engagement. Most importantly, I was able to fulfill my business goal of making a difference in society, even if only a small one. A network is an entrepreneur's greatest asset. It is never too late, or too early, to start, so perfect your pitch and start making introductions within your market.

6 WEEK FAST-TRACK CHALLENGE

Launching your own business can be more than a little overwhelming. That is why I have created the 6 Week Fast-Track Challenge to help guide you through the process. Now hold on to the seat of your pants. This six-week challenge will have you working day in and day out, investing much-needed time into creating your work-life dream. If you are trying to make your dream a reality alongside of working another job, no worries, extend the challenge to 12 weeks to give yourself time to properly brainstorm and strategize for success.

WEEK 1: The Personal Work

Day 1: Get a Journal

Head on over to your local stationery or office supply store and pick up a journal. Don't just purchase a notebook, choose a journal that is inspiring. You will be recording a very big step in your life within these pages. This journal will serve as your transformation into an unconventional entrepreneur. It is not necessary, but if you would like to jazz up your journal, pick up some highlighters, colored pens, and motivational stickers as well.

Day 2: Take the 8 Elements Personal Evaluation

Take the *8 Elements Personal Evaluation* in Chapter 3 and record your top three and bottom three elements in your journal. Also, to prepare for the Discovery Kit activity, schedule a minimum of three interviews with family or friends to be conducted over the phone or in person on day three.

Day 3: Complete the Discovery Kit

Print the Discovery Kit from Chapter 6 and conduct interviews with family or friends to get an outsider's perspective on your talents and skill set. Then, complete the Self-Evaluation Worksheet within the Discovery Kit to become more grounded in your passion and business ideas. Did any light bulbs go off? Was there any surprising feedback from your peers? Record these "ah ha" moments in your journal.

Day 4: Determination and Confidence Check

Complete the worksheet in Chapter 7. Further evaluate your level of determination and confidence within your journal. Also, express your concerns and excitement when it comes to this venture. As the challenge goes on, you will refer to this journal excerpt to evaluate how your feelings, fears, or reservations have changed.

Day 5: Plan Activities for Improvement

Once you have uncovered your weaknesses within the 8 Elements, plan activities to work on these weaknesses for improvement. In Chapter 5, you will find several personal development activities to steer you in the right direction. Plan four activities to be completed on Days 7, 14, 22, and 35.

Day 6: Rest and Reflection

Doing personal work can take a lot out of you. While praise always feels good, constructive criticism can be a hard pill to swallow. Today I want you to turn off and take a self-care day. You are going to need the break before tackling the next part in the challenge as you will be going full steam ahead on developing and bringing your work-life passion to fruition.

Day 7: Activity 1 for Improvement

On Day 5 you planned four activities to help improve upon your skillset within the 8 Elements. Today you will spend time completing the first activity.

WEEK 2: Brand Development I

Day 8: You as the Expert

We discussed the importance of branding yourself as a trusted expert within your field. Research ways that you can build upon your professional portfolio. Perhaps there are online accredited courses available, industry specific podcasts that would have you on as a guest, local magazines that would like to publish an editorial piece on you, etc. In your journal, record any accredited courses or conferences that you are interested in attending. On a separate page, list local and national media outlets that you would like to target in your public relations strategy. *(To learn more on creating and launching a PR strategy, check out my The Unconventional Entrepreneur course.)*

Day 9: 4 Senses Strategy in Action

Complete the *4 Senses Strategy in Action,* activity in Chapter 10. Using the answers from this worksheet, write a short story about your brand. Be sure to include your brand's voice, personality, colors, adjectives, and imagined smell. This marks the beginning of the brand visualization process.

Day 10: Explore Your Environment

Now, we will start to bring elements of your brand into the real world. Using all the information you have gathered from the 4 Senses Strategy and the story you created on Day 9 involving your brand, set out on a 4 Sense Strategy adventure.

First, head on over to your local candle or fragrance shop and activate your olfactory senses by experiencing different scents and recording, in your journal, those that fit your brand vision.

Next, visit local stores and explore their environments while also taking note of their company color schemes, fonts, logos, and textiles. Does the experience match the brand visual? In your journal, record your positive and negative observations, as well as some ideas for your brand visuals. Last, create a playlist that embodies the sound of your brand.

Day 11: Develop Your Vision Board

Using all the tools you have learned from the 4 Senses Strategy activities, create a vision board. I like to use old magazines, stickers, scrapbook paper, rhinestones, etc. for making an inspiring, eye-catching vision board. Hang your masterpiece in an area that you will pass by daily so that it can be easily admired. This will help you to keep your eyes on the prize.

Day 12: Brainstorm Brand Names

Today, you will use your vision board to complete the, *Name That Brand*, activity in chapter 11. This will help you to brainstorm brand names and create a list of your top favorites. Record the list in your journal. (*For my exclusive, printable Brand Guide, check out The Unconventional Entrepreneur course.*)

Day 13: Secure Your Brand Name

You will need to check availability of your top brand names to be sure they are not already in use. Complete the three steps for checking brand name availability at the end of Chapter 11.

Day 14: Activity 2 for Improvement

On Day 5, you planned four activities to help improve upon your skillset within the 8 Elements. Today you will spend time completing the second activity.

Notes:

_____
_____
_____
_____
_____
_____
_____
_____
_____
_____

WEEK 3: Brand Development II

Day 15: Logo Design

Today you will review your journal entries from week two and begin your logo design. Many entrepreneurs choose to work with an experienced graphic designer and others choose to design their own logos. (*For more logo design resources, check out The Unconventional Entrepreneur course.*)

Day 16: Top of the Week Reflection

Today you will spend time reflecting on all that you have accomplished in the first 15 days. Record your thoughts, wins, concerns, and project progress within your journal. Reflect on your Day 4 journal entry on determination and confidence. Has anything changed? Do you feel more determined and confident? Do you feel overwhelmed? Record your thoughts and feelings.

Day 17: Pitch Development

Complete the, *Constructing Your Elevator Pitch* activity from Chapter 12. When listing ways that your business will solve your clients' problems, do a little extra competitive research. How is your competition solving their clients' problems? Record your research within your journal. This will help you to develop a competitive edge with your elevator pitch.

Day 18: Perfect Your Pitch

Today you will practice your pitch to perfection. First, you must look the part. Get ready as if you are going to a conference or networking event. Stand in front of a full-length mirror and practice reciting your pitch until you have it memorized. Notice your facial expressions and hand gestures. Do you look inviting, friendly, and trustworthy? If there is something about your pitch that just doesn't feel natural, now would be the time to reconstruct your pitch so that it flows eloquently from your tongue.

Day 19: Shoot for the Stars

Before you dive into the activities in Chapter 13, spend time imagining the greatest successes that may lie ahead. In your journal, record all your aspirations, goals, and projected outcomes for this journey. Nothing is off-limits, even if it is a bit unattainable. Today we dream big! In the following days, we streamline our dreams into attainability.

Day 20: Personal Reflection

Print and complete the *Personal Reflections Chart* activity from Chapter 13. Refer to your journal entry from yesterday. What may be keeping you from achieving these goals?

Day 21: Goal Attainment

Print and complete the *Goal Attainment Worksheet* from Chapter 13. Refer to your journal entry from Day 19 and strategize to include some of the more immediate goals. These are the goals that are met through processes that can be easily worked into your daily routine for quick goal attainment. This doesn't mean that you should forget about all your other aspirations and goals. A wise man once told me, *"Shoot the alligator closest to you."* Once you have achieved your initial goals, you can revisit your Goal Attainment Worksheet to add goals from Day 19 that didn't make the first cut.

WEEK 4: Networking

Day 22: Activity 3 for Improvement

On Day 5 you planned four activities to help improve upon your skillset within the 8 Elements. Today you will spend time completing the third activity.

Day 23: Developing the Tangibles

Soon, you will begin to build your network for business success, but before doing so, you will need to have business cards and personal profiles, or media kits on hand. Spend time creating show-stopping materials for making a memorable first impression while networking.

Day 24: Capturing Colleague and Client Contact Information

When networking at events or delivering an elevator pitch, you will likely gather colleague or client contact information. It would be a grave mistake not to record this information in a digital database for follow up and future use. Today, you will set up two separate databases, one for colleague contacts and the other for client information. (*For more strategies on database set-up and lead generation, check out The Unconventional Entrepreneur course.*)

Day 25: Plan to Network
Research networking events, conferences, or mentorship groups. Plan to attend at least three events, conferences, or group meetings this month. Be sure to bring your business cards and follow up with any important contacts within three days of the event.

Day 26: Outreach

Attending events and meetings isn't the only way to network. Head on over to Google and research successful local entrepreneurs to introduce yourself. Once you have established a relationship, maybe you can discuss ways to work together for mutual success. You can also research entrepreneurs who are in the same industry but in a non-competing market. While some may be a bit hesitant to divulge their success secrets, many will admire your enthusiasm for the industry and be happy to give advice. I recommend first reaching out via email, and then setting up a quick call for further introduction.

Day 27: Bottom of the Week Reflection

Today you will spend time reflecting on all that you have accomplished in the past 27 days. Record your thoughts, wins, concerns, and project progress within your journal. Go back to past reflections in your journal and notice any positive changes and personal developments. Record all your thoughts and feelings on your unconventional journey thus far.

Day 28: Self-Care Day

I bet you were wondering when another one of these would come along. By now you know that there is a lot that goes in to becoming an unconventional entrepreneur and you are well on your way! Take some time today to relax, meditate, soak in your tub, or do anything that brings you peace. This day is about self-gratification.

WEEK 5: Reaching the Market

Day 29: Who is Your Market?

Now it's time to dive back in, but this time, from your customer's viewpoint. Today you will define your target market. In Chapter 15, we go over the five generations active in the marketplace today. Use Google to research your target demographic further by gathering more detailed information on your target market's purchase behaviors, social and societal viewpoints, and consumption habits. (*For more tools and a streamlined strategy for pinpointing your target demographic, check out The Unconventional Entrepreneur course.*)

Day 30: Choose Your Market Mediums

In Chapter 15, we reviewed several mediums for both conducting business and bringing your brand to your customer. In your journal, choose the top mediums in which your brand should be present.

Day 31: Create an Omnichannel Blueprint

Once you have decided on the mediums for brand exposure and business operations, you will need to plan how each of these mediums will work together to create the ultimate omnichannel experience. Do some of these platforms integrate with one another? Are there specific technologies that are available for streamlining a digital and personal experience? (*For my exclusive Digital Blueprint, check out The* Unconventional Entrepreneur course.)

Days 32-34: Platform Set-Up

For the next three days, you will work on setting up your digital platforms. This includes your website or online shop, blog, social platforms, mobile apps, email newsletter host, and any other digital brand presence. *(For detailed strategy and setup, check out The Unconventional Entrepreneur course.)*

Day 35: Activity 4 for Improvement

On Day 5 you planned four activities to help improve upon your skillset within the 8 Elements. Today you will spend time completing the fourth activity.

Notes:

_____

_____

_____

_____

_____

_____

_____

_____

_____

_____

WEEK 6: Pricing For Profit

Day 36: Top of the Week Reflection

Today you will spend time reflecting on all that you have accomplished in the first 36 days. Record your thoughts, wins, concerns, and project progress within your journal. What are some unique and unexpected ideas that you have come across through this process? Do you feel like you have improved upon your 8 Elements through this journey? What are some lingering concerns?

Day 37: Price Your Product/Service

In Chapter 14, we went through the P.R.O.F.I.T. Cost Process. Today you will consider only the costs involved with the production of your product or service. *(If you are not producing a product to be resold, use today to review Chapter 14 for the following challenge days.)* In your journal, make a list of all production costs involved in your operation.

Day 38: Competitive Price Analysis

Complete the *Competitive Price Point Analysis* activity in Chapter 14. Create a pricing scale for your products and services based on this analysis.

Day 39: Create Cost Lists

Consider the overt *(variable)* and fixed costs that will be associated with your business. In your journal, begin creating two budgets. The first budget will list all your projected fixed costs. You can estimate these costs by doing local rental and utility cost research, as well as other internet searches to average out your costs of doing business.

The second budget sheet will list your variable costs. As with your fixed costs, you can use the internet to average these costs as well. For example, average labor wages in your industry and state. Always round up when listing costs. It is better to expect to pay more than to round down and underestimate your total cost of doing business. These lists will help you when it comes time to make investment and budgeting decisions.

Day 40: Determine Your Worth

In Chapter 14 we also talked about your impact cost. Review this section of the chapter and assign an impact cost to your expertise.

Day 41: Pricing Structure

Now that you have assigned costs to your production activities, established your variable and fixed costs, completed a competitive price analysis, and determined your impact cost, it is time to define your total margin markup and package up your pricing structure. Research industry standards to establish your margins. For example, in the book industry, average margins are set at 50-55%; in other industries, your margins can be much higher at 100%. Determine what your profit margins will be set at and create a menu for your products or services.

Day 42: Final Reflection

This last reflection is to give yourself a huge pat on the back. Through this process, I am sure you have learned a lot about yourself and your passion. In this final journal entry of the 6 Week Fast-Track Challenge, record a few new facts you have learned about yourself since becoming an unconventional entrepreneur. What have you improved upon?

How has your business idea evolved through the development process?

While this may be your last journal entry in the challenge, this is only the beginning of your unconventional story. Keep your journal with you through this new and exciting journey. Record the unbelievable tales, roller coaster rides of events, and most importantly, your life-changing experiences and unconventional lessons. This will be one of your greatest adventures.

Notes:

_____
_____
_____
_____
_____

BONUS WEEK 7: Launch Power

Ready to launch your work-life dream but need help with the next steps? In my course, The Unconventional Entrepreneur, I will walk you through the process of launch planning to successfully introduce your business to the world.
Visit ***www.learnunconventional.com*** for more information.

WHAT'S NEXT?

While this book has come to an end, your journey as an unconventional entrepreneur has just begun! In the final chapters of this book, I have included a list of my Unconventional Wisdom axioms and a 6 Week Fast-Track Challenge for taking your business aspirations from an unconventional idea to a full-blown brand launch. If you would like to further your education beyond this book in the 8 Elements, branding, digital media, lead generation, and more strategies for launching a successful business, scan the QR code below and sign up for my course, The Unconventional Entrepreneur, in my online school, The UE Academy. *(www.learnunconventional.com)*

The course is packed with topics such as:

- Mastering The 8 Elements
- The UE Brand Guide
- Digital Blueprint
- Lead Generation
- Launch Power

Because mastering the 8 Elements is such an important piece for business success, Part 1 of my course offers refresher activities from this book. The following four sections in the course provide detailed information for launching your public relations strategy; a digital blueprint for setting up branded websites, online stores, and social platforms, step-by-step instructions for developing successful lead generation strategies that convert to profit and email automation for keeping your brand front and center; as well as initial launch "how-tos," expert advice, exclusive new printables, and many more resources so that you can launch a successful business and live your work-life dream!

Scan the Code

UNCONVENTIONAL WISDOM

While I don't claim to know it all *(Does anyone actually ever know it all?),* here are some tidbits of unconventional wisdom that I have picked up during my journey in business. Some of these axioms have come from other incredible unconventional entrepreneurs and mentors, but most are personal concepts I developed when reflecting on difficult situations that I have faced during my journey as a business owner. Feel free to adapt these to fit your personal experiences or add new unconventional wisdom to the list!

- You can't eat if you can't hunt.

- You can't win them all.

- If you are going to make it as an entrepreneur, keep one thing in mind, nothing is beneath you. Let your moral compass be your guide. Determination, even in the midst of hopelessness, is key. And always keep your eye fixed on the end goal.

- Always remain proactive. Building in time to act proactively in your business is more productive than falling victim to chasing chores reactively.

- One of the beautiful things of being an unconventional entrepreneur is the fluidity of structure, yet this fluidity often brings about uncertainty which makes way for new opportunity. And with every new opportunity, risk-taking is warranted to seize that moment.

- Your business is a play and you are the puppet master. When you temporarily remove yourself from the plot and observe the landscape outside of the narrative, learning will ensue. This will allow you to clearly recognize new opportunities on the horizon and broaden your perspective.

- You only have one life to live. You can choose to carry on in mediocrity or go bravely into the unknown and seize all that life has to offer.

- Exist in many worlds.

- Remove failure from your mindset.

- The moment you take an idea from your brain and execute it in the external world, it exists outside of you and reaches a level of tangibility.

- Become a brand that excites the senses.

- Experience is the evolution of brand and business.

- Just like an award-winning choir must perfect their pitch, so must the successful entrepreneur.

- Do not neglect, yet perfect and respect.

- Nothing is beneath you.

- Never tip the scales

- Learn to get out of your own way while also knowing when to pull back on the reins.

- Stay in your lane.

- Be kind to yourself.

- Be more than just a business, be the expert.

- Keep the omnichannel top of mind.

ACKNOWLEDGMENTS

This book has been several years in the making, and I couldn't have done it without the love and support of my husband, Greg. Thank you so much for spending many of your nights after work, listening to my ideas, helping to edit chapters, and being so understanding and patient when my time and focus were dedicated to this project. I am so lucky that I have you to do life with. You are my rock, my love, and my best friend. I love you, Beau.

To my children, I am so blessed to be your mother. I often reflect on the role you all have given me and I always come back to the same thing. *You are my purpose. You will never be able to understand how you have saved me.* You all are my number one. When things get tough, I remember why I am here, to give you the best life I can, to love and snuggle you, to remind you that you are always enough, and be your rock in life. You keep me going. I love you all more than you will ever know.

To my parents, thank you for always supporting my wild and crazy dreams, being there to pick me up when I fall, and cheering me on as I navigate through this journey. I love you guys!

Daddy J., watching you operate and own several companies while I was growing up has been such an inspiration. I admire your business success and continuously strive to be just like you. I am such a proud daughter and am so very lucky to call you my dad. I love you so very much!

Daddy P., you have always been my number one fan. You constantly remind me that I can take on anything that life throws my way. Not a day goes by that I don't think about, how lucky I am to have you in my life, not only because "You are the smartest man in the world," but because the love and support you have given me is out of this world. I love you!

Mama K., "I am woman, hear me roar." I remember you jokingly saying that phrase to me as a child, and I would repeat it and laugh. That phrase is so true to the way you have raised me and to who you are. As the strong, corporate woman that you are, I have always looked up to your successes and have leaned on you several times throughout the years for business advice and guidance. Thank you for always being there for me. I love you, mom!

Mama S., I remember when starting my very first business at the age of 17, you gave me my first $100 to get started. Throughout the years, I have shared so many crazy business ideas with you and without hesitation, you are always there to rally for me and support me, just as you did when I was a little girl. I love you to heaven and back, and back again!

To my brother and sister, and "partners in crime," a life without you would have only been half fulfilled. What a lucky girl I am to have such incredible siblings to have learned with and leaned on as we grew into adults. You have always believed in me and backed me up. Even though I am the oldest, and by nature, had the job of being the role model, I have looked up to both of you and admired you so much in life. I love you guys very much. Thank you for being my very first best friends.

To my friends, I am so blessed to have such an amazing, authentic group of girls. You have always supported me and continue to be there for me in all of my ups and downs. I am so grateful for your encouragement, advice, and love.

To my publisher, designer, and editor, thank you for making my dream of becoming an author come true. This experience has been incredible. Because of you, this book has come to fruition. I am forever grateful for your hard work, advice, and care in making this publication everything I had hoped it to be.

To all the followers, fans, and readers, without you, none of this would have been possible. Every word of encouragement and constructive criticism has been greatly appreciated. Your continued support has allowed me to live this life fulfilled as an *unconventional entrepreneur*. Thank you for giving me encouragement and the means to pursue my dreams. Thank you for coming on this journey with me!

REFERENCES

Berger, Jonah and Chip Heath (2007), "Where Consumers Diverge from Others: Identity Signaling and Product Domains," Journal of Consumer Research, 34 (2), 121- 134.

Campbell, Margaret C. and Linda L. Price (2021), "Three Themes for the Future of Brands in a Changing Consumer Marketplace," Journal of Consumer Research, 48, p 517-525.

Confidence. 2022. In Oxford Lexico. Retrieved June 20, 2022, from https://www.lexico.com/definition/confidence

Determined. 2022. In Britannica.com. Retrieved July 10, 2022, from https://www.britannica.com/dictionary/determined

Digital Marketing Institute. (2021, October). 20 Surprising Marketing Influencer Statistics. Digital Marketing Institute. https://digitalmarketinginstitute.com/blog/20-influencer-marketing-statistics-that-will-surprise-you

Grohmann et al, (2012),"Using Type Font Characteristics to Communicate Brand Personality of New Brands," Journal of Brand Management, 20 (5), 389-403.

Hsu, Jeremy. (2010, June 24). Just a Touch Can Influence Thoughts and Decisions. https://www.livescience.com/8360-touch-influence-thoughts-decisions.html

Impact. 2022. In Oxford Lexico. Retrieved June 20, 2022, from https://www.lexico.co m/definition/impact

Khattak et al. (2018), "Color Psychology in Marketing," Journal of Business and Tourism, 4(1), 183-190.

Lee, R. M., & Robbins, S. B. (1995). Measuring Belongingness: The Social Connectedness and the Social Assurance scales. Journal of Counseling Psychology, 42(2), 232–24.

Manifest. 2022. In Merriam-Webster.com. Retrieved June 20, 2022, from https://www. merriam-webster.com/dictionary/manifest

Mind Tools Content Team. Golden Rules of Goal Setting: Five Rules to Set Yourself Up for Success. Mind Tools. Retrieved May 21, 2022, from https://www.mindtools.com/ pages/article/newHTE_90.html

Morley, L. (2021, March 30) Our guide to marketing to different generations: A Step-By- Step Guide. Business Clan. https://businessclan.com/how-to-market-to-different-ge nerations-a-step-by-step-guide/

Hustler. 2022. In Oxford Lexico. Retrieved June 1, 2022, from https://www.lexico.com/definition/hustler

Passion. 2022. In Oxford Languages. Retrieved June 20, 2022, from https://www.oxfordreference.com/definition/passion

Process. 2022. In Oxford Lexico. Retrieved June 20, 2022, from https://www.lexico.com/definition/process

Profit. 2022. In Oxford Lexico. Retrieved June 20, 2022, from https://www.lexico.com/definition/profit

Skill. 2022. In Merriam-Webster.com. Retrieved June 2, 2022 from https://www.merriam-webster.com/dictionary/skill

Tai, J. (2021, January 19). Council Post: Startup Surge: Pandemic Causes New Businesses To Double. Forbes. https://www.forbes.com/sites/theyec/2021/01/20/startup-surge-pandemic-causes-new-businesses-to-double/

TechTarget. (2020,October14). What is omnichannel? -Definition fromWhatIs.com. Search Customer Experience. https://www.techtarget.com/searchcustomerexperience/definition/omnichannel

Terwogt, Mark M. and Jan B. Hoeksma (1995). "Colors and Emotions: Preferences and Combinations," The Journal of General Psychology, 122 (1), 5-17.

Trait. 2022. In Merriam-Webster.com. Retrieved June 2, 2022 from https://www.merriam-webster.com/dictionary/trait

ABOUT THE AUTHOR

Alexandra Nolan is a self-made digital entrepreneur and mom of three from Memphis, Tennessee. She is the founder of City Chic Living blog and CEO of The UE Academy. Alexandra obtained her MBA from the University of Memphis and studied International Business Studies at Bournemouth University in England.

Alexandra has appeared in "Forbes," was named on Yahoo's "Most Inspiring Influencers" list and has been featured in many other notable national publications. She is a published guest columnist and women empowerment speaker, dedicating her work to inspiring and uplifting entrepreneurs who seek to be empowered through an unconventional lifestyle and the exploration of their environment and the world in which they live.

When she is not mentoring other business owners, you will find her with her family, making memories with her husband and children, playing with her pups, and enjoying time with friends.

Follow along in Alexandra's journey through her social media accounts and on her blog, City Chic Living.

⊡ @alexandra.nicole

⊡ @learnunconventional

🌐 www.citychicliving.com

CPSIA information can be obtained
at www.ICGtesting.com
Printed in the USA
BVHW052330090223
658265BV00015B/355/J